Redefining More Able Education

Redefining More Able Education is an essential, up to date and challenging introduction to the many factors involved in teaching more able students. Written by Ian Warwick, founder of London Gifted and Talented, and Ray Speakman, this book challenges our understanding of provision for the more able and explores ways in which we can ensure that students reach their full potential.

Providing a thorough overview of topical research, the book offers a range of practical solutions for engaging students and encouraging them to become more independent in their learning. Warwick and Speakman explore key ideas including differentiation, resilience and motivation, and unpick issues including the history of more able education, the relationship between intelligence and achievement, working with marginalised groups and how students can overcome barriers when applying to top universities. A dedicated chapter summarises 21 easy-to-implement strategies that can make a real difference to teaching practice.

This definitive guide to more able education will be essential reading for teachers, school leaders and any education professionals reflecting on different approaches to motivating and teaching the more able in order to better provide for all their students.

Ian Warwick is the founder and Senior Director of London Gifted and Talented (www.londongt.org) which has worked with more than 3500 schools internationally. An inner-city teacher for 20 years, he has published extensively in the field of education and has written award-winning high-challenge e-learning materials and several film screenplays.

Ray Speakman founded the Birmingham Youth Theatre, has edited and written plays for schools, professional theatre and television, and was a teacher of English and a deputy headteacher in a large Warwickshire comprehensive.

Redefining More Able Education

Series Editor: Ian Warwick
London Gifted and Talented

For more information about this series, please visit www.routledge.com/Redefining-More-Able-Education/book-series/RMAE

Redefining More Able Education

Key Issues for Schools

Ian Warwick and
Ray Speakman

Routledge
Taylor & Francis Group

LONDON AND NEW YORK

First published 2018
by Routledge
2 Park Square, Milton Park, Abingdon, Oxon OX14 4RN

and by Routledge
711 Third Avenue, New York, NY 10017

Routledge is an imprint of the Taylor & Francis Group, an informa business

British Library Cataloguing in Publication Data
A catalogue record for this book is available from the British Library

Library of Congress Cataloging in Publication Data
A catalog record for this book has been requested

ISBN: 978-0-8153-5310-2 (hbk)
ISBN: 978-0-8153-5311-9 (pbk)
ISBN: 978-1-351-13730-0 (ebk)

Typeset in Bembo and Gill Sans
by Florence Production Ltd, Stoodleigh, Devon, UK

Ian and Ray would both like to thank their respective wives and children for their patience, support and love during the writing of this book.

Contents

Preview

Inside out

The arrangement of the chapters in this book takes a cue from the Pixar animation *Inside Out* (2015), in that our *redefinition* of more able education comes in two parts: the outer and the inner landscapes that make up the world of an able child.

Part One (Chapters 1–7) is the 'outer world' of our subject and it describes all those busy *big* people who give the topic its context: governments, schools, inspectors as well as the international perspectives that influence what we do. We include those other influential aspects in any society – the long shadows cast by disadvantage and poverty. Also, we discuss (and *unforget*) all those ideas that have informed our understanding of the more able, such as intelligence, character and the principles we think should inform and drive what happens in schools. As William Gibson the writer once commented, *The future is already here; it's just not very evenly distributed* (1999). However much we promote equal opportunity, inclusive classrooms and schools, we still find that equality is elusive. So the first part explores the worldwide overarching 'external to school' type factors that influence how more able education is perceived by society, where it may have gone astray in the past, what some of the common misconceptions might be, which students tend to struggle most, and what parents can and can't really do about it.

Part Two (Chapters 8–14) moves away from all those busy big people in the outside world towards the busy *little* people inside the heads of able learners: how they deal with what happens in their classrooms, how issues of motivation can interfere with learners' mental furniture, how teaching strategies such as differentiation help or otherwise, and the importance of encouraging independence. Just as the Pixar film is about how physical and psychic landscapes interact, *Redefining More Able Education* attempts a similar symmetry. We finish with a look at higher education – and why some commentators believe it is in crisis. Two quite extensive lists make up the final chapters: *21 ways to shape a whole school culture*, and a *Glossary of ideas*. These have informed our approach and offer an opportunity to share that alchemy of ideas which have inspired us. We argue throughout this book that putting all your eggs in the basket of one theory or another misses the opportunity to see theories, not in a binary way, but as a series of complex and dynamic interactions.

In the end, we hope to promote a sort of collective reasoning that does **not** conclude with, *here is the answer, do this and all will be well*, but rather allows us to rediscover, re-evaluate, recombine those ideas, theories and experiences in a multi-dimensional attempt to find individual solutions for individual learners. After all, for us as teachers, it has to be about individuals just as much as learning has for each of us always been a personal and an individual matter. Learning has delivered us to ourselves – who we are and what we have or will become, and this is what we hope it will do for those we teach.

References

Docter, Pete and del Carmen, Ronnie (dirs.). *Inside Out*; 2015.
Gibson, William; *Talk to the Nation*; radio talk, 1999.

Part one

Chapter I

Introduction

What to take on board?

Recently, a worldwide survey asked practitioners concerned with provision for the more able to identify what they saw as their main problems (Freeman, Raffan, and Warwick, 2010). Their responses were dominated by the practical ways they felt that their work was being short-changed by a lack of funding, training, capacity, time, teacher skills, interest, space, resources, ideas and technology. Beyond that, and in terms of the way their work was seen and understood, they complained of being regarded as advocates or agents of some outdated and immoral educational apartheid system. Consequently, they and those students they hoped to lead towards high performance felt misperceived and side-lined.

Those were their main worries, but there are more.

There is an increasingly evident phenomenon called, 'PISA shock'. This is when a country's education system is plunged into crisis by the publication of that country's ranking by the Programme of International Student Assessment. The assessment measures mostly mathematics, reading and science, with a small amount of problem-solving and financial literacy. Many argue that since these assessments began, education systems across the world have dramatically increased their reliance on quantitative testing. Education has become about testing and finding ways to move up the PISA rankings. Some would argue that we have become nations of league tables – which are easy to sensationalise and which make unfair comparisons between very different societies. PISA offers, critics say, a single, narrow, biased yardstick, a 'testing juggernaut', a global testing regime that has become a sort of educational colonialism led by an organisation which appears to have become the arbiter of the means and ends of education around the world. These tables have become something of a Bible on absolute standards for various governments across the world and not least, for the media – a perfect weapon with which to beat teachers over the head. We do not have to rehearse the figures here, they are readily available – but we do have to say that it's too easy to dismiss these figures as coming only from crammer/sweat-shop type jurisdictions. Whatever the approaches elsewhere and however much we might disapprove, we have to concede that many other countries seem to take the education of their most able students much more seriously than we do in the UK. That should worry us.

Like Jude Fawley in Hardy's *Jude the Obscure*, we are encouraged to believe that there is a 'prescription' or a 'secret cipher' possessed by some other countries, and if we could only find it then we too would hold the key to the top spots on the PISA lists. Jude calls it the law of transmutation, a belief that someone out there holds the key to success and all we have to do is persuade them to hand it over and all will fall into place. Applied to education this leads to what we can only describe as educational tourism, which is about looking at those countries that regularly shine on the PISA lists, such as Finland and Singapore, for answers. Politicians and the media seem not to notice that other countries not only have other education systems but also different cultures. Finland, for instance, is a relatively wealthy society with a population of 5m, and a fair degree of cultural homogeneity. Similarly, Asian and Eastern European countries might seem to be succeeding because they view the most able as an elite who need to be taught as a special needs group, but in some of these countries this former certainty is now being challenged, and concerns have grown about the way hot-housing and an impressive command of basic principles seems to have been achieved at the expense of creativity and originality. In yet other countries, there are no programmes for the more able at all. For about two thirds of the world's population such programmes would be a luxury and beyond what their education systems could offer as standard. In western cultures, an interest or lack of interest in the more able students has tended to be a political rather than an educational issue. Stephen and Warwick (2015) observe that *renewed attention . . . tends to follow on from a crisis* and they cite as examples the perceived need in the USA to compete more *successfully* in the space race in the 1950s, and later, the shortage of home-grown science, technology, engineering and mathematics (STEM) specialists. Is it beginning to look as though the more able agenda is in danger of becoming *a feather for every wind that blows* (Shakespeare, *The Winter's Tale*)?

And for those teaching in the UK, the worries do not stop there.

About every two years the UK's inspection processes throws up a report which generates headlines such as: '*Schools not doing enough to support most able students*'. In general terms, they say, many state schools do not provide sufficient challenge for all students, but particularly for the more able: '*thousands of highly performing primary pupils are not realising their early promise when they move to secondary school*' is one of Ofsted's headline conclusions (2015). If this is true in many schools, they found that it is particularly the case where students are from poorer backgrounds, or if they are boys, or how they perform when they first enter secondary education. A second organisation, The Sutton Trust, dedicated to increasing social mobility through raising student aspirations has also expressed its concern over provision for the more able. It finds schools complacent and Government policy (or lack of policy) moving towards '*ever less comprehensible measures*' (they don't seem to make sense). It's not just that we are not taking the education of the more able seriously enough, as Ofsted and The Sutton Trust are telling us loudly and clearly, many schools simply do not recognise those students who have the potential to become high performers. We seem to have forgotten that the early twenty-first-century attempts in the UK to foreground and develop an education system which recognised and nurtured the more able was initiated with the with clear and precise intention of making state education truly comprehensive.

Sir Peter Lampi, chairman of the Sutton Trust, says in response to data about the performance of more able students in the UK: '*These are shocking findings that raise profound concerns about how well we support our most academically able pupils, from non-privileged backgrounds . . . these figures show that few bright non-privileged students reach their academic potential – which is unfair and a tragedy for them and the country as a whole*' (2012). He goes on to say that to condemn the less able to a similar lack of recognition would be seen as morally unacceptable and yet we seem to find it okay to side-line the more able. This perception will touch a nerve for many of us who have taught in the UK's comprehensive system, where the needs of the most able have for the most part simply not been met, and because those students complain less, and often just get on with their own education as best they can, their needs have never become a whole school priority. It is a peculiar form of egalitarianism which states that *equal* opportunity is the same as everyone having the *same* opportunity.

Even more to think about

The global survey we opened this chapter with (*Worldwide Provision*) told us about more than a dearth of practical provision, and a feeling that the agenda is frowned upon by many inside and outside the profession. Put these things together with the findings of Ofsted and The Sutton Trust in the UK and it becomes obvious that it would be an act of denial to make an ostrich blush if we, and some other countries too, tried to pretend that we are doing well regarding our most able students. We clearly are not. Either some nations take the education of their most able much more seriously than others or apparently they know something we don't know. For the sake of these students we clearly need to wise up to the resulting waste of our national talent.

As well as practicalities and attitudes, the survey also touched on the theories about how best to respond to high ability, which of those theories are most and least in vogue, and how beliefs are shifting – one way or the other.

The survey's respondents perceive a steady movement *away* from more able education designed in terms of high ability as predominantly inherited – and therefore, for the most part, unchangeable. Even though some scientists are finding growing evidence that degrees of intelligence *can* be identified in DNA, many educationalists are more and more saying that, *IQ doesn't matter* (Berliner and Eyre, 2017)· In practical terms, this means that withdrawal for acceleration or special provision has declined and able children are more likely to be taught alongside all other children. Some would see this as an inclusive approach, others as an invitation to the more able to perform below capacity. The nature of high ability, too, has been questioned. It is now seen to be as much about character as it is about IQ, and as a consequence it can be taught. Place this in a context of a well thought-through programme of enrichment and effective differentiation in the classroom then what had become in some quarters an elitist programme of provision has morphed into ways of teaching the more able that is believed to be less restrictive, less separatist, less elitist. In short, conscientiousness is winning in the race against a reliance on IQ in order to access what Hardy's Jude saw as the key to success. One final perception about the way things are going: given the variations in the profile of the more able in different countries and in different schools, and in the consequent levels of provision, teachers seem to be looking to fill the void by seeking out local, national and international collaboration as a way of staying in touch with the agenda and doing the best they can for their charges. The more able agenda is not going to go away, nor are teachers going to stop worrying, thinking and talking about it.

So, what do we believe? Where do those beliefs come from? Is there a theory or an all-embracing approach that we can hold on to? The social psychologist, Herbert Crovitz, said that: *Theories do two things: they account for the data, (or) and they make people happy* (qtd. in Engel 2011). Despite the obvious impact of PISA data, particularly on governments, there has been a general move away from theories built from data and a move towards theories that make people happy. Data from PISA, SATs, and IQ tests draw teachers towards an approach that shapes – even dictates – the way we teach. Tests such as these offer quantifiable measures of potential and achievement – and perhaps most of all, what appears to be hard evidence of how well a school or a country is doing. Niccolo Machiavelli would have approved of the way such tests have come to dominate thinking and practice – a means to rule by fear and distraction, one of the key strategies developed in *The Prince*. He would have understood the phrase we use several times in this book, 'anxious literalism'. We are so concerned that our students do well in the tests, that how to take tests is what we teach – often at the expense of a whole tranche of other classroom endeavours. When teachers are criticised for marginalising creativity, problem-solving, wider reading, the arts, for dampening aspirations and side-lining enjoyment – Machiavelli would have joined with all those other critics of schools to say that no one *told* teachers to drop these other pursuits and focus almost entirely on test preparation – it was their own decision.[1] Those who oversee education try to deny breadth and choice without actually saying that they are denying breadth and choice.

Crovitz sets data-related theories against that broad range of approaches which do their best to make people happy. Howard Gardner's theory of multiple intelligence would fall into that latter category (1984). As Engel points out, Gardner's egalitarian theories of intelligence have been used by teachers to make *all* children feel that they have some form of intelligence about which they can feel good. Parents, teachers and students feel happy when they can believe that it is possible to improve intelligence, when nurture is in the ascendant over nature, when environment has a clear advantage over genetics. Teachers would take this a stage further: they express scepticism not only about the way tests can be used as a once and forever measure of promise, but also in the way they use a practice known as *norming*, that is, deciding how well or otherwise a child does in a test compared with other children (or children in other countries) so that they do not measure the child as an individual but in relation to the average levels of achievement in that age group.

We argue throughout this book that putting all your eggs in the basket of one theory or another misses the opportunity to see theories not in a binary way, but as a series of complex and dynamic interactions. It seems obvious to us that a child's home and school environment has a huge influence on how that child progresses and it might also seem that a child's environment is readily open to change and development. However, that environment can also have the opposite effect, it can be hugely difficult to influence and change – as we see later when we talk about disadvantage and 'walls in the head'. Similarly, a child's apparently 'fixed' inclinations towards particular skills, as revealed in a test for instance, can be enhanced or squashed by that child's circumstances at home, in society or a particular school. Environment and quantifiable abilities are not so much in opposition as they might first appear.

Theoretical alchemies

> If we are not constantly rethinking ideas, we are not really thinking.
>
> (Poole, 2016)

This idea from Steven Poole makes a key point. Ideas do not stand still. They are always on the move; a *process* rather than a finished thing. Similarly, in relation to recognising and responding to the needs of more able learners, the practicalities, the theories and the

realities continue to evolve, and as this series of books will show, are still on the m/
Endeavours to establish a definitive approach gained considerable traction in the /
years of the twenty-first century, but those intentions have in more recent times retreateu
into the corners of our classrooms. We expected that once defined, the whys and
wherefores of this aspect of teaching and learning would develop in a linear way and
lead towards a consensus and a common approach in our schools. As Ofsted in the UK
says repeatedly, it has not happened; from their point of view it would appear to be a
combination of wilfulness and apathy on the part of schools. The Sutton Trust would
argue that schools either do not understand the more able, or the approach they have
been persuaded to adopt has led them to bark up the wrong tree.

The contest now seems to be between a focus on the certainty offered by testing and
a conviction that learners can be made smarter by other means – mostly to do with
character development.

If Poole is right in his view that ideas are a *moving target*, we should have expected
this ebb and flow of theory to be the case. Not that we think that one or the other idea
alone should dominate our thinking and our practice, or that all those earlier theories
about the pedagogy of challenge and raising expectations are now irrelevant and should
be forgotten. This and the books that follow in the series should at least encourage us
to see how some of those ideas might be justified in being *unforgotten*. Re-encountered;
redefined; refreshed. Poole uses a French saying to make his more general point about
not being too quick to abandon the past: *reculer pour mieux sauter* – if you begin by taking
a step back, you will jump further.

Words into actions

Having made the case for looking for those ways in which theories and approaches
interact and feed off each other, and how the past can often inform the present, it is only
fair to report that this is not what teachers said in the survey. The survey provided a
useful opportunity for some to vent their frustrations, but apart from telling us what they
see as wrong with the ways things are, they were also telling us, or somebody, about
what they think needs to be done about the situation.

This is what they think we need to take on board:

1. We need to build a capacity across education systems to respond to the needs of the
    more able. Initial training and professional development need to focus on the skills
    to deliver effective classroom differentiation (see Chapter 9).
2. We need to recognise that the more able population should broadly reflect the
    whole school population. It is essential to take a multi-faceted approach to discovering
    hidden potential. Open access approaches are still unusual (see Chapters 3 and 8).
3. Whole school improvement is enhanced by a focus on more able education. There
    is often too much emphasis on improvement from the bottom up, tackling the needs
    of the lowest achievers. By informing curricular and pastoral approaches with the
    needs of their most able learners, schools can create a much more positive environ-
    ment in which diversity and innovation are valued. This is rewarding for the whole
    school community, and for teachers as much as pupils and parents (see Chapters 2
    and 13).
4. Classroom teaching can be provided through acceleration, enrichment and differ-
    entiation – determined by the needs of the learners. Acceleration and enrichment

are not mutually exclusive and a rich approach to provision will incorporate elements of both as appropriate (see Chapters 9 and 11).

5. Diversity means that one size will *not* fit all. Although it may be tempting to assume that more able learners are similar, these students are as diverse as the general pupil population. It follows that providers must tailor their provision to suit the very different needs of the individual learners (see Chapter 5).

6. Educational effects of disadvantage must be recognised. There is a growing international focus on inclusion. Recognising high-level potential in disadvantaged learners brings more able education into mainstream educational practice (see Chapters 5, 6, 7 and 11).

7. Parental engagement is critical to effective provision. Some of the most recent publications on nurturing high ability recognise the centrality of the importance of parents to a child's learning (see Chapter 7).[2]

8. Online programmes can support improved collaboration and communication as well as strengthening student learning and professional development (Allison and Tharby, 2015).

9. Evaluation is imperative. Providers must carefully and continuously monitor outcomes of the learning they offer, so that issues can be spotted quickly and problems rectified. Evaluation is important evidence to support the case for expansion or replication of a service elsewhere. Many providers are aware of the importance of evaluation, but too few are translating that into practice (see Chapter 12).

10. Research needs to be robust and supportive, and expressed in terms that are meaningful and relevant to practitioners (see Chapters 1 and 14).

Plenty to talk about?

Throughout the survey the respondents insisted that they needed to constantly ask themselves the following questions:

School-wide procedural issues: Is there a plan? How do we make it happen and where is it heading? Is high achievement a wall or a doorway in the head of our students? How do we know and record what's happening?

Classroom strategies: Are we working on strategies to enhance subject-specialised challenges, including opportunities for genuine problem-solving? Vertical grouping, enrichment and acceleration? Participation in challenging real-world competitions? Are we providing opportunities for any student to shine?

Involving and nurturing teachers: Are teachers involved and trained? Do they have regular access to further professional training and certification? Do they have online and live support for longer-term effective training?

Partnerships beyond school: Can we form networks with like-minded schools? Can we improve access to good facilities and get volunteers from outside school? Are we seeking expertise from beyond the school and bringing in graduates and researchers? Are we using the internet and finding specifically designed online multimedia resources?

Involvement of stakeholders: How are parents involved to support the work? Are we building effective communication networks with all key stakeholders? Working closely with leadership teams and governors within the school? Working *not* to neglect public opinion?

The use of student voices: Do we listen carefully to what students tell us about what they like and want? Do we have a school council with real responsibilities?

The world at large: Do we lobby governments? Seek advocates? Apply for long-term funding? Get scholarships for our students?

Learning becomes who we are

For us, learning came for the most part from books or a teacher and has *developed* from what we have read or heard. When that learning has impact, it becomes part of a sort of everlasting present tense; in relation to what we have learned we are always *in media res* – in the middle of things. It is not a fleeting experience. It will always have an immediacy; it will always be there. It can be third-person – shaped and driven by a teacher or an examination syllabus (or even an IQ assessment, or PISA and SATs data) – or it can be first-person – arising from the social and emotional needs of individuals, but once the learning has happened it becomes part of who 'we' are in the widest possible sense. It becomes **first-person plural**. What students encounter in or because of the classroom experience thus becomes part of themselves and by implication part of our collective understanding of who we are in relation to one another.

That's why what we do is so important – and it shouldn't be that complicated:

> If people working together can design a space programme that sends humans to the Moon and robots to Mars, it doesn't seem all that difficult for people working together to design a school curriculum that will give the best chance of a decent education to everyone.
>
> (Poole, 2016)

Which of course begs the question, what exactly do we mean by a *decent education*. If this and the other books in the series have a common thread it is that: a *decent* education. The science fiction writer William Gibson used a phrase that sets some hares running through this and all the books in this series: *The future is already here; it's just not very evenly distributed* (1999). However much we promote equal opportunity, inclusive classrooms and schools, we still find that equality is elusive, which is why the implications of that phrase *evenly distributed* require our urgent attention.

Treating everyone the same, or offering equal *access* to learning, might suggest that we think equal access means that everyone receives the *same* education. We would argue for a more precise application of the phrase, *even distribution*. If what is on offer does not find a connection with a learner's individuality, then whatever level of potential they might possess is artificially impaired by our insistence that everyone is the same. However, if the learning experience matches the capacities of the learner, they will stand some sort of chance of maximising whatever potential they might have. This is how we would want to read the phrase, *evenly distributed* – not standardised provision, but rather, personalised or differentiated provision. This is exactly why we make such a fuss throughout the series about differentiation and why it's so important in our classrooms. Differentiation challenges the idea that all children are the same and encourages us to teach *to the edges* rather than to the middle; it promotes student-centred, self-paced, alternative routes; it's about, in that earlier educational rallying cry – which we will now declare unforgotten – *excellence for all*. What we mean is excellence for each learner in all the various ways that the individual learner *finds* and *defines* their own version of excellence.

How does this happen? Do we seem to be suggesting when we talk about learners finding and defining their own pathways that we are proposing to reincarnate Rousseau's Emile who received, *no verbal lessons* but would *only be taught by experience alone* (1762)? Throughout these books we use Pierre Bourdieu's phrase, *cultural capital* as shorthand for what we believe teachers and parents provide. Of course, we embrace curiosity, learning through experience and the powerful possibilities offered by serendipity, but we also recognise that adults *prime the pump* of learning. Ian Leslie's metaphor expresses this neatly: *If children are to become wise and skilful operators of the cultural vehicle into which they have been born, we need to help them locate the controls* (2014). We should provide able learners with those *associative networks of understanding* so that their *cognitive bandwidth* might be widened.

It will no doubt become clear throughout this and the books that follow that this approach is our approach too. This book and those that follow are all about chasing down those associative networks of understanding so that we might widen our own cognitive bandwidth, our own understanding of more able learners so that they achieve the best possible version of who they might become.

Notes

1. This idea comes from a Michael Rosen article in *The Guardian* (June 2016) where he argues that Government denies alternatives to teachers without actually saying that they do not have alternatives.
2. See Berliner and Eyre *Great Minds and How to Grow Them*; Routledge 2017; Susan Engel *The Hungry Mind*; Harvard 2015; Paul Tough *How Children Succeed; Grit, Curiosity and the Hidden Power of Character*; Random House 2012.

References

Allison, Shaun and Tharby, Andy: *Making Every Lesson Count*; Carmarthen, UK: Crown House Publishing 2015.

Berliner and Eyre: *Great Minds and How to Grow Them*; Oxford: Routledge 2017.

Engel, Susan: *Red Flags or Red Herrings?*; New York: Atria 2011.

Engel, Susan: *The Hungry Mind*; Cambridge, MA: Harvard 2015.

Freeman, J., Raffan, J. and Warwick, I.: *Worldwide Provision to Develop Gifts and Talents: An International Survey*. Reading: CfBT Educational Trust 2010. Accessible from www.londongt.org.

Gardner, Howard: *Frames of Mind*; New York: Basic Books 1984.

Gibson, William: *Talk to the Nation*; radio talk 1999.

Leslie, Ian: *Curiosity*; London: Quercus 2014.

Machiavelli, N.: *The Prince*; London: Penguin Classics, 2003.

Poole, Steven: *Rethink: The Surprising History of New Ideas*; New York: Random House 2016.

Rosen, Michael: *The Guardian*, June 2016.

Rousseau, Jean-Jacques: *Emile (or On Education)*; New York: Basic Books 1979 [1762].

Shakespeare: *A Winter's Tale*; Ware, UK: Wordsworth Classic 1995.

Stephen, Martin and Warwick, Ian: *Educating the More Able Student*; Thousand Oaks, CA: Sage 2015.

Sutton Trust, The: *Educating the Highly Able*. 2012. Available at: www.suttontrust.com/research-paper/educating-the-highly-able-2/.

Tough, Paul: *How Children Succeed: Grit, Curiosity and the Hidden Power of Character*; New York: Random House 2012.

Chapter 2

Framing more able education
Baggage check?

In the UK, Ofsted have done their best to keep high ability on the school agenda and to focus on how much of the teaching experienced by the more able often results in lacklustre progress. In two quite thorough reports, in 2013 and 2015, they point out that the most able students in non-selective schools are not achieving anywhere near as well as they should, that there is too little focus on academic excellence and that students get used to performing at a far lower level than they are capable of achieving. The Chief Inspector of Schools at the time of these reports, Sir Michael Wilshaw, said that what they found painted *a bleak picture of under-achievement and unfulfilled potential. Thousands of our most able secondary-age children are still not doing as well as they should* (Ofsted, 2013). We would argue, from our experience worldwide, that this is not a problem only in non-selective UK education, and that drawing attention to the issue is not just about how we meet the needs of the most able. How able students experience their schooling is a touchstone or an indicator of how well or otherwise schools meet the needs of all children – as this trenchant remark from Wilshaw makes clear:

> How well the brightest children are doing will usually be among the very first questions an inspector asks the school leadership team at the start of the visit. This is because inspectors know that if provision for this group is good, it is likely that other groups of pupils are also being well served. Conversely, if the most able pupils are not being stretched, that will alert inspectors to the possibility that things may be going wrong elsewhere.
>
> (Ofsted, 2013)

As our parents would have said to us when we were children, *when are you going to do as you're told*? Why is there what appears to be a wilful neglect of some students in some schools in the UK? Could it be that the UK has developed a squeamishness about recognising and developing high ability students? When we run sessions in schools we occasionally feel obliged to do a 'baggage check' exercise in which we ask teachers to 'declare the issues' that the participants may have about more able education. We feel we have to check these issues in before the journey starts so that the baggage doesn't slow down the training. That way we can get on with the teaching and learning. This is done with the promise that if they still feel similarly about the issues by the end of the day, we will examine them in detail at that point. They don't.

The two writers of this book have well over fifty years in inner-city teaching, working as an integral part of the London Challenge, local and regional partnerships and as inspectors and subject advisors. In those roles, we have run training with a focus on Special Educational Needs, English as an Additional Language, isolated learners in rural settings, looked after children, and Black and Minority Ethnic students, but never once have either of us felt the need to run such a 'check in' service. It's automatically assumed that if you are dealing with these students, then of course their needs should be met. It would be criminally negligent not to do so. And yet, as Ofsted says, the needs of the more able are frequently ignored, as if somehow their needs are less important or are somehow a betrayal of our commitment to equality.

A very brief story from the United States Airforce in the 1940s would help us make our point. Pilots were finding the cockpits of their planes increasingly difficult to manage. Earlier research had shown that what was needed was a design that fitted the physical needs of the average pilot. The result was that the cockpits fitted no one. There was no such pilot as an average pilot. Eventually, a junior researcher suggested that the cockpit need to fit *every* pilot rather than the *average*. He proposed adjustable seats – just like the ones in all modern cars. In classrooms, there is no such thing as a middle way to fit the average student, and the worst form of that inequality we are afraid of is to try to make unequal things equal. Meeting the needs of able students still carries with it that faint whiff of elitism, that sense of a 'robbing Peter to pay Paul' and the 'Matthew' effect of accumulated advantage – to those that have, more shall be given.

If a junior researcher into cockpit design can adjust to the needs of unique individuals, so can we. A focus on the more able is absolutely an equal opportunities agenda, one which we hope to address this throughout this book.

What does the baggage check reveal and is there a way to respond?

If teachers at training sessions were not such a polite and gentle group of people they would probably say or think something like this:

> Resources should be focused on the genuinely needy with real problems, who cannot cope without our explicit support. Besides, if we focus on the smart students it raises all kinds of divisions between all of our classes. All identified More Able students look a little like Hermione Granger, come from middle class supportive families, and would basically succeed no matter what the school did because their snowplough parents will put all the backup strategies into place to ensure that in the event of a nuclear fallout, they will still be doing pretty well, thank you very much. Private tutoring, taking them out to see culturally interesting exhibitions and artefacts, yet more private tutoring and sometimes even discussing issues with them face to face. No wonder they can't fail.

Except of course they do fail. All too frequently. And worldwide, on an industrial scale. Even these 'heavily supported' students often go off the rails, or misunderstand the demands being made of them or the degree of difficulty of the exam, or assume that because they might be top of their class they will automatically get the top grades they need. Sometimes the anxiety that expectation can produce simply cripples them.

But we all know that these students are just the tip of the iceberg. The straightforward reality is that the very children who need some of the greatest support because they are smart but disadvantaged are precisely the able students who are most likely to under achieve. They don't get to go to the cultural events, don't get to hear the right word spoken at home, don't have their parents (or anyone else) helicoptering in when they start to slip and slide. They are the ones we need to support the most in school, or their talent will be squandered, their aspirations abandoned and their future blighted. Ofsted suggest that these are the children who are not getting the support they require, not getting access to the pupil premium and not achieving anything like their potential. This is the core of the equity agenda. It is by far the most powerful argument to get colleagues genuinely engaged.

Arguments about whether or how able children ought to be identified, and how that process promotes divisions and antagonisms between them, are laughable. Every child in every class can you give you a pretty accurate list of exactly who is good at what subject. The divisions are already there and totally apparent – and children are very good at spotting cover-ups. For teachers to pretend that all children are the same makes them look foolish. We are not arguing, of course, that only the more able are important, we are just arguing that these students are *also* important. And pretending that intelligence doesn't predict success (which we will explore later) doesn't make that seemingly uncomfortable fact go away.

There is, though another problem: *lists* and the fixation that some schools have on creating concrete lists and the accompanying cultural or social goodies that go only to those on the lists. A sure way to effectively design teacher, parental and student opposition to any scheme. A rotating door identification process or a talent pool approach based on tests, observations, teacher assessments and even professional hunches is far more effective. The focus on top end challenge being offered in every classroom in every lesson renders the need for the 'top up enrichments' that cause such resentment almost totally redundant. What then happens to these students is far more significant than being able to point to them. And the focus on more able provision is also far more likely to get colleagues on board.

Framing a language of effective provision for the more able

The highest of ambition for our students is all too often sacrificed on the altar of convenience. As Goethe said, '*if you treat people as they are, you will be instrumental in keeping them as they are. If you treat them as they could be, you will help them become what they ought to be*' (2013). There is an evocative and instantly recognizable phrase to describe the UK's (and no doubt many other nations') national obsession with grade boundaries, levels and league tables. The phrase is **anxious literalism**. It implies that we work with such a frantic level of conscientiousness that we effectively install a 'glass ceiling' over learning. We tend to teach to the tests and worry when students do not seem to be working at the required or predicted level. We forget individuals; we think of them as a limited set of scores and anything outside that we treat exactly as we would a typo. The truth is that no student can be reduced to a couple of test scores, but in our anxious literalism perhaps we sidestep the very top end students because *they'll get there anyway, won't they?* If the learning environment we provide does not accommodate individuality, then every aspect of that student's performance will be constrained. If we are to convince students that learning is worthwhile and that they might benefit from studying a subject further, then we need to teach beyond exam requirements and explore the threshold concepts that promote absorption and excitement. Of which, more later.

It is difficult for able students to genuinely understand what excellence and scholarship might look like, for them to appreciate what a subject explains or offers to the world, if we insist on feeding them only bite-sized, easily digested chunks. We need to talk explicitly about subject mastery and not gloss over the big issues and complex concepts in our subject. Learners are experts in development and we have to come clean about the fact that becoming an expert is about challenge and struggle. We don't have to spell this out in mini-lectures or inspirational posters on the wall, we simply have to model high level immersion in the subject specific language we use in our teaching – by avoiding synonyms and dumbing down. When we are clear in our expectations regarding the accuracy and precision of the technical language we use, we are making it clear that precision is expected and this feeds a high level of thought and debate.

If we are continually making our challenging demands explicit and are raising the bar through rigorous feedback to their extended and reasoned answers, then we have at the same time to teach them to expect and to deal with failure. We have to ensure that it is productive failure.

The forces on teachers can be both contradictory and crippling. As a result, we can often challenge and doubt the very nature of what we are doing. Should it be to get a struggling student to floor level targets, or to inspire a highly able student to think like an expert? Outside influences can be very powerful. We are susceptible on a daily basis to exam board nihilism, to government diktats or to bite-sized reductionism. These pressures often mean that we are willing to accept short-term performance from students rather than focus on long-term scholarship – and take 'refuge' in easy, learned answers. These are outcomes devoutly to be resisted.

How can we turn doubts and concerns into a rallying call for the more able?

According to Saul Bellow, '*knowing things allows us to open the universe a little more*' (1982). At the same time learning brings us to ourselves. Effectively managed and delivered it will remain part of who the learner is. How do we make this happen, and what is more, how do we persuade our colleagues that such an endeavour offers to return us to what excited us about our subjects in the first place, and at the same time make us all better teachers? Sir Michael Wilshaw pointed out that thinking through policy and provision for able students provides us with the perfect lens through which to view more clearly the needs of all our students. It's also a way of really looking closely to see how well we accommodate individuality in our classrooms. The most recent Ofsted Reports seem to suggest that we do not do it all that well. Later we will look at setting and streaming but for now suffice to say that the thought of trying to make the classroom environment fit each student – rather than making each student fit the classroom environment – fills many teachers with a deep, deep feeling of weariness. Yet, there is no avoiding what Ofsted has told us repeatedly – there is no mythical middle ground. Aiming materials at that middle, in the hope somehow that the top and bottom ends can find their own level, and the more able create their own stretch and challenge, is a forlorn hope. It's an approach that effectively implies differentiation by outcome. Which simply means no differentiation at all, as it merely requires the teacher and the students to turn up.

This agenda needs the support of colleagues – hence this series of books; without the support of other teachers our attempts at sharpening policy and provision for the more able will be side-lined. The conversation needs to be framed in terms of 'access to high challenge'. This isn't the same as saying equal access – that's aiming at the middle again. If our role is reduced to the gatekeeper of the register, then our influence and impact will be pretty minimal. With clear support we are far more likely to have impact, meet the governors and be called in to management meetings to add our voice to the key dialogues.

Launching our case with a 'low threshold high challenge' agenda for all students is a pretty good rallying call across most schools.

Talking to groups of more able students about what they enjoy, which lessons stretch and challenge them, and where they see their aspirations taking them, means that we can appeal to colleagues in a far more specific and personal way. They will quite instinctively rally around an individual student who needs extra support. We should speak to parents too, so that we have a clearer idea what their concerns might be. It helps to clarify and adjust our beliefs and thereby our strategies, and it also serves as a useful source of evidence to lay alongside some of Ofsted's observations and enquiries. A useful balancing voice can be generated by interviewing interested colleagues about how they are raising expectations and achievement. By doing this it triangulates our evidence as well as personalising our able education agenda, and that in itself can encourage colleagues to engage. Teachers respond brilliantly to individual cases far more than they do to imposed causes, or even worse, the latest trundling initiatives.

By keeping more able policies simple and sustainable (preferably by stating a few key 'manifesto' beliefs), it means that colleagues see what matters to the education of the more able matters to them, too. The most obvious element that needs to be included is that the best provision for the more able occurs in classrooms (not after school or in holiday enrichments) through targeted differentiation of materials and tasks. This starts to become a school's vision for what it wants to achieve working with the most able students, and it won't then be seen as 'yet more' for teachers to have to deal with. This needs to be informed by a clear definition of what 'more able' means in the context of any specific school and critically each department, but with a flexible and inclusive 'talent pool' or 'revolving door' approach to identification. Start with a clear focus on equal opportunities and meeting the needs of all students. If all this is done early on, then colleagues' concerns are immediately side-stepped and the focus moves quickly moved on to provision: a far more fertile territory in most schools. Teachers will instinctively engage with something that they can really put their hearts into and which makes a difference to the lives of their students – not endless squabbles over who should or should not be on the register, which is genuinely pointless, not to mention, a pain, a diversion and a mistake.

More able education should remind colleagues why they became teachers in the first place simply by helping to take them away from the various borderline 'dead zones' that obsess the many of the powers that be and that no one ever went into teaching to focus on. Done well, it reinforces teachers' perception of learners' potential, it can restore the pride in the achievement that teachers rightly feel – achievements that various governments have done their best to knock out of them with repeated pronouncements on how dreadful everything is in our schools. It's our time to ignore various political masters standing in the shadows and spitting at the sunlight and simply use the talents of our more able students to help us restore some pride and professionalism.

By setting higher levels of challenge and stretch in the tasks we set, in the questions we ask, in the expectations we have of how much our students will cover in and beyond our lessons, we change their perception of what is possible for them to achieve. For our more able students, a longer narrative arc means teachers have an increased opportunity to think deeply about the pace of teaching and learning; this means from the outset of the school year, and in every lesson (and beyond-lesson work), setting a pace that genuinely challenges students and moves their learning on rapidly by capitalising on every possible opportunity for widening their understanding. It also means the chance to think about pace of recall, and how we can ensure that our students are able to secure and consolidate their understanding.

The implications for teacher expertise

Teacher expertise is quite simply the key. What helps students to love a subject and to want to study it further? 'Off-piste' lessons that go beyond the syllabus requirements inevitably create a sense that there is so much more to learn, which is vitally important for igniting our students' passion, thirst and enjoyment for learning. Finding ways to take our more able students beyond the confines of the syllabus is critically important. When learning for learning's sake and learning as its own reward start to become the norm, this lays the foundations for building a culture of scholarship that our more able students need if they are to thrive and survive at the highest level of study in school and beyond. It is also critically important in such off-piste excursions that we refine the way we use questions, that we look at the purpose as well as the types of questions we ask, so that our more able students are continually being engaged and making progress in their learning. The questions we ask and the questions we seek from our students need to be both cognitively challenging and able to progress students' understanding. This needs to happen as a matter of course so that higher-order, open-ended questions are used to create opportunities to fully open learning.

We need to understand the purpose and function of any subject we teach as fully as we can to help our students develop their own clarity and passion. Expertise is more than the quality and quantity of what we know. It is also hidden inside the more specialised ways of thinking that become the language of instruction that we use and share. We are obliged to be Vygotsky's 'more knowledgeable other' ready and willing to provide learners with the necessary linguistic fingerprint of words and ideas so that they might have the equipment they need to answer the challenging 'why' and 'how' questions we throw at them. Every teacher needs a thorough understanding of his or her subject and must know how to communicate that understanding. The quality of our teaching is likely to be one of the most important factors in how much our students learn, and without doubt we need more intellectual heft in the profession, based on the simple principle that no one can teach what they don't know. Highly educated teachers tend to choose material that is more rigorous and challenging and are less threatened by student questioning.

There are big ideas and troublesome knowledge in every subject domain that only an expert teacher can deliver to students. All of this expertise takes time to acquire and at present, certainly in the UK, there is little requirement for staff to refresh their subject knowledge regularly as they move through their careers. But without this our student's own journeys to subject mastery are likely to be damaged. There are many ways to keep this up: taking out (and using) subject-specific journal subscriptions in order to keep up-to-date with latest developments and thinking; undergoing masters and doctorates; setting up research reading groups; mutual observations within departments focused on promoting independent learning; teaching-focused department meetings looking at high-end differentiation strategies; departmental meeting time that specifically includes opportunities for developing each other's subject expertise; and a rich department website for sharing resources among many others and creating a bank of subject knowledge podcasts.

Our job is vitally important and there are many ways we can demonstrate to our more able students that we understand and can support them: by not rewarding their second-best endeavours and ensuring feedback is only given on their best work; by encouraging bravery by taking risks yourself in the classroom and by talking about your own less than perfect learning journey to expertise; and by anticipating likely student misconceptions, interrogating and challenging their responses and by not allowing ourselves to become the only thinker and questioner in the classroom. But perhaps most of all by demonstrating your love for your subject. It is sometimes easier to stretch and accelerate our more able students than it is to keep them on the journey with us. As teachers, we sometimes forget that we have become experts in our subjects. We get used to 'explaining' key concepts and the more difficult areas of our domains, but we neglect to explain to our students what it is that we found emotionally engaging about our subject in the first place – why we chose to study it and what we feel it is there to explain. So it is really helpful to use personal anecdotes, stories and epiphanies in our classroom to support our students to understand why it is meaningful. That includes making it clear that there are moments where we still get excited about our subject and why that happens. It also means that we should explain to students what helped us to 'get' our subject, our own learning histories and where our sense of security and expertise comes from.

A lack of ambition and ignition?

There is a research industry out there seeking, perhaps, to justify its own existence by focusing on all the 'traits' of the most able students that require attention and support. A casual glance at the attention put on over-excitabilities, vulnerabilities and burn outs (perhaps all adding to the 'freaks and geeks' perception of ability) suggests that there are a great number of researchers professionally fretting over children that they see as being 'crippled by their ability'. While it would be foolish to suggest that this is never the case, many of these anxieties are sometimes caused by over-anxiety from parents and educators on the lookout for any signs of weakness or discomfort. The fear is often about students 'burning-out'. To use an analogy, the blend of fuel used for racing is tuned for the demands of different circuits – or even different weather conditions. More potent fuels give noticeably more power but that needs to be balanced against the danger of engine wear. However, it has to be acknowledged that the lack of demand made by the curriculum across much of the system is that students have far too few challenging circuits to negotiate. Put simply, the lack of ignition is a far more serious problem in UK schools than the risk of burning out. On a daily basis, schools face students who have lowered their sights, lost commitment and ambition, and acquiesced to turgid spoon feeding and easy successes. Students constantly under-challenged, being given material they have already mastered, often caused by a rigid adherence to the basic core curriculum, has created boredom on an industrial scale (for both teachers and students). The following of a lukewarm 'set quota of knowledge' set by the faceless demands of the low-level syllabus only, has resulted in a loss of passion and a seismic disengagement that is surely the single biggest threat to aspiration.

How should we set sights high for enrichment and extension tasks?

I believe that work of excellence is transformational. Once a student sees that he or she is capable of excellence, that student is never quite the same. There is a new self-image, a new notion of possibility. There is an appetite for excellence. After students have had a taste of excellence, they're never quite satisfied with less; they're always hungry.

(Berger, 2003)

Often schools will comment that they are catering to the needs of their most able students by offering them a 'free choice' in their enrichment or extension work. Sometimes this looks like a selection of ever increasing challenges which are offered as a smorgasbord of activities. At other times, it is a completely free and open choice with no suggestions or steers given for fear of 'leading the learning'. The problem with the former is obvious. This becomes known as differentiation or enrichment by punishment. Well done, you're smart. Here is some more, harder work, without the reasons for why a student may want to choose this being explained. When offered a choice that will involve a little work and another that requires a great deal more work, some students are inclined to choose the former, even if the latter is more interesting, often because these are usually the students with a great number of other pressing demands on their time. Or sometimes because being bright doesn't mean you aren't sometimes lazy. The problem with the latter is that it can be bewildering and use up great gobbets of displacement time while the students try to work out what it is that they are meant to do. It can also have the exact opposite impact of stretch and challenge with students who underestimate what they are capable of achieving and who sell themselves short.

What is most important is that enquiry and discovery are hugely significant and powerful elements of learning in any compacted or accelerated scheme. That is not to say that sometimes a clear helicopter overview of our teaching intentions across a course will go amiss. Able students often want the big picture to clarify where they are and what they have embarked upon. There's no contradiction between having a map and enjoying being on the actual ground.

But we also need them to like the stimulation of wrestling with unforeseen obstacles and problems, particularly if this involves anomalies that undermine comfortable assumptions. We want to stimulate their enjoyment of ambiguity, complexity and uncertainty, speculating on what isn't there, what remains to be discovered. They need to know, and their teachers need to understand, that education is not only about finding the answers; just as exciting is finding the questions. We need to concentrate on what

our subject still cannot answer and examine why things are still uncertain. It wou
to design deliberate disorientation into your lessons to enable students to b
defamiliarised and have to cope with and make sense of these experiences. And w
take risks ourselves.

References

Bellow, Saul: *The Dean's December*, 1982.
Berger, Ron: *An Ethic of Excellence*; Portsmouth, NH: Heinemann Educational Books 2003.
Goethe, Johann: *Wilhelm Meister's Apprenticeship; A Novel*; TheClassics.us 2013.
Ofsted: *The Most Able Students: Are They Doing as Well as they Should in our Non-Selective Secondary Schools?* 2013.

Chapter 3

History's mislaid ideas
Lost property?

The ears, the heart and the mind have their own shape for each individual.

(Okri, 2009)

An agenda for the more able?

We began with a fair degree of puzzlement, not to say frustration, about exactly *why* all that has been written and said about the more able over the past twenty years or so seems to have slipped off the shelves, out of earshot and into the archives. On reading the title of this chapter, 'an agenda for the more able', there will be those who bark back, *whose agenda?* All we can say, and we have already said it in the opening chapter, is that it's an agenda driven by individual students and their needs. Sometime ago the Labour Government argued that giving every single child the chance to be the best they can be, whatever their talent or background, was not a betrayal of excellence; it was the fulfilment of it. It is not elitism to nurture 'the best', just as it isn't condescension to support those with learning disabilities. It's what we do as teachers: we champion difference and resist sameness; we see individuals, not data, or types, or backgrounds.

The Sutton Trust (2012) point to the construct '*gifted and talented*'[1] being *at the root of the problem* and how that label for the more able is rather precious and embarrassing to students, as well as teachers, because it suggests 'better' rather than 'different'. The minefield around methods for the identification of potential high ability – *so many ways and no set way* – has not helped. Throw into the mix uncertain leadership, the ever-present fear of undermining equality and a weekly influx of other 'solve everything' agendas which promise to make everything okay, and we begin to understand why there is so much 'baggage' around the subject.

Yet, despite the pleas of uncertainty and confusion, the UK schools' inspection process has been unequivocal and unrelenting about how more able students are being short-changed by their education. The logic is clear: if one group of students are not being adequately dealt with, then other groups of students are also in danger of being overlooked and denied a response to their learning needs.

In 2013 and 2015, following numerous school visits and inspections, the UK's inspectors (Ofsted) published two reports, both of which asked the same direct question: Have schools taken any notice of all those urgings by the UK's National Strategies, School Inspectors and others to develop and embed an agenda to meet the needs of more able students?

The first of these reports, called *The Most Able Students*, appeared in June 2013. The terse headline to this report insisted that: the most able students in non-selective secondary schools are not achieving as well as they should. By way of evidence the report noted that: 65% of pupils who achieved a Level 5 in both English and mathematics at the end of Year 6 failed to attain A or A★ grades in both these subjects at GCSE in 2012 in non-selective schools; leaders in our secondary schools had not done enough to create a culture of scholastic excellence, where the highest achievement in academic work is recognised as vitally important; and students arriving in secondary schools had not been subject to anything like an effective or comprehensive transition process. At Key Stage 3 (11 to 14 year olds) teaching took little account of the more able, so that most students became used to performing at a lower level than they are capable of and this seemed to be accepted by teachers and parents; the curriculum and the quality of homework required improvement; inequalities between different groups of the most able students were not being tackled satisfactorily; assessment, tracking and targeting were not being used sufficiently well in most schools and too few schools worked with families to support them in overcoming the cultural and financial obstacles that stood in the way of the most able students attending university. In fact, most of the 11–18 range of schools visited were insufficiently focused on university entrance, and schools' expertise in and knowledge about how to apply to the most prestigious universities was not always current and relevant.

Two years later, in 2015, Ofsted revisited the question – using the same title, *The Most Able Students*, but then adding with more than a touch of irony given what they found, that this new report was *an update on progress*. The tone of the headline to this report had moved from the polite description of the more able as, *not doing as well as they should*, to the increasingly frustrated, *still being let down*, which in turn leads to a failure to reach full potential. As a result, nationally, too many more able students failed to achieve the grades they needed to get into top universities. Secondary schools were not making anything like adequate use of transition information from primary schools; they were rarely meeting the distinct needs of students who were more able and disadvantaged; leaders had not embedded an ethos in which academic excellence was championed with sufficient urgency; as in the earlier report 11 to 14 year olds were particularly badly served by a curriculum and teaching that lacked challenge. Information, advice and guidance to students about accessing the most appropriate courses and universities were not good enough; while leaders made stronger links with universities to provide disadvantaged students in Key Stages 4 and 5 with a wider range of experiences, they were not evaluating the impact sharply enough. Assessment, performance tracking and target setting for more able students in Key Stage 4 were generally good, but were not effective enough in Key Stage 3. Because of all this the inspection process promised to sharpen its focus on the progress and quality of teaching of the more able students.

This second report added several more detailed observations on the way the 11–14 age group (Key Stage 3) is let down by schools. Many students in this age group are set adrift in a sort of educational doldrums from which many higher ability learners do not recover. This loss of direction starts with missed opportunities at transition from the earlier stages of a child's education and leads into a world where there is lacklustre progress, waning academic ambition, an assumption that the stronger teachers are needed elsewhere, a failure to address the needs of the disadvantaged and to get parents on board, teachers not being adequately trained in how to introduce high challenge into their classrooms, a lack of robust teacher and curriculum evaluation and a failure of school leadership to recognise the issue and look beyond the school for support.

In short there is evidence (not entirely universal, we would hope) that: primary and secondary schools are not talking to each other; the first three years in a new school are a black hole of lethargy; the curriculum sags; teaching drifts; by the time we really need the students to up their game for external examinations (and the league tables) they have lost the plot, their 'cultural capital' is threadbare and their appetite for hard work has ebbed away. As for university – no, not really.

The 2015 Ofsted report concludes with a terse instruction that everyone – schools, the government and Ofsted itself – need to pay attention to these issues! We write this almost three years later. How much has changed?

What is the problem?

Between 1997 and 2010, the now defunct National Strategies *were* paying attention to the needs of the more able in an extended series of guidance booklets and self-evaluation templates, all aimed at drawing our attention to the issue, widening our understanding and giving us practical help in turning theory into classroom practice. Yet Ofsted has found, twice, that all this undeniable diligence has *not* had the necessary impact.

The Sutton Trust argue that the problem has been **the name** we gave to the most able, 'gifted and talented'. They call it a *confusing and catch-all construct* that has *taken policy makers down a number of blind alleys* (2012). The suggestion is that the phrase failed to achieve an accepted definition: 'gifts' and 'talents' never quite reached stable meanings for teachers, psychologists, school leaders or politicians, let alone students and their parents. As result, the Sutton Trust recommends that our focus should quite simply be on those learners *capable of excellence in school subjects*, and it calls those learners *the highly able*.

So – we ditch the former name and call these learners, the *highly able*, (or maybe the more able – as we do in this series of books) but we then collide with the next big problem: Who are they? How do we identify them? We touch on this discussion in the chapter on Intelligence, but the Sutton Trust argue that current Performance Tables[2], which measure attainment at the end of Key Stage 2[3] in terms of 'high', 'low' or 'performing at expected level' are far too imprecise, *spanning the highly able to those just above average*. Their recommendation is that a highly able learner should be defined by KS2 test results[4] and if we were to follow what happens in places such as Singapore and South Korea, this would mean the top 1% nationally. When there was in the UK a national policy for identifying, and compiling a register listing such students, (1997 – 2010) the expectation was that something like 5–10% would be included *in each school*. The stumbling block for the Sutton Trust is the huge differences between schools in terms of intake. The solution, they say, *is to create a numerical map showing which primary schools they are in, and to which secondary schools they should go* (2012). They say that in identifying the more able in these ways, *we do not envisage that they would be placed in a box and other pupils excluded. The prime purpose is to ensure that the highly able are not neglected* (2012). Despite this last reassurance, many teachers would be unsettled, sceptical even, of the Sutton Trust approach. It is an approach that makes it easy for some to replace the word 'excellence' with the word 'elitist', or to dismiss any possibility of high achievers from disadvantaged backgrounds, or to do exactly what Ofsted perceives we

do far too much of – concentrate most of our efforts at the thresholds between w'
considered a 'pass' and what a 'fail' rather than embracing high challenge in wh
teach and how we teach it. In the end, how you see all this depends, we would su_{gg}
on whether you see the prime purpose of schools as being to *educate* children, or to *sort*
them according to ability.

We talked earlier about 'recognising' exceptional ability. A way through the problems
of names and identification is to see beyond *measuring* ability and to think about how
we might *create ability* (Hymer, Whitehead & Huxtable, 2008). According to this
approach, 'gifts' are *made* not found. It is about promoting an approach in our subject
that *anticipates*, rather than simply recognises, excellence – and anticipation is about
providing a high challenge curriculum and classroom climate that provokes and supports
high achievement. As we shall see later, when learners experience such an environment,
they begin *to see* themselves as able; they define themselves not by the races they have
lost, but the ones they have won – a way of seeing that a successful athlete would
endorse.

For Hymer *et al.*, what happens in our lessons is about the future as well as the past.
It is about how learners integrate past knowledge with current experiences. Established
ability, genes, social background, proven intelligence might well provide an 'objective'
measure of ability but they should not be used to exclude some learners from encounters
and opportunities that might transform them. As Deborah Eyre pointed out, those
learners we see as markedly able: *are simply the most effective learners, not a specific, clearly*
defined, sub-set of the population with learning needs so unique that they cannot be accommodated
through normal, recognised teaching approaches (2008).

Learning is not just about 'what is' but also about what 'might be' (Rosen, 2016).

The principles behind the agenda

We ask again, behind whose agenda? The first time we asked the questions we said it
was an agenda which responded to the needs of more able students. The second time
of asking, we would want to broaden the answer. It's about our needs, as teachers. It's
not just about what our work in classrooms should *look like* (Ofsted has told us that) it's
about *how* we get it to look like that. It's about those core, often life-belt, principles
which inform the work in the classroom and which for a few minutes anyway, we need
to set aside from the demands of the world of governments, examination boards and
what appears to be global competition. What is it that drives us to teach and students to
learn? After the results day, the job application, higher education and a career, what
remains? How has learning delivered us to ourselves; has it, in other words, delivered us
to who we are and who we want to be?

When the learning experienced in the classroom has impact, it becomes part of a
sort of everlasting present tense. It is not a fleeting experience. It will always have
an immediacy; it will always be there. The writer Graham Swift says that narrative
may be written in the first- or third-person singular, but once it 'happens' to the reader
it becomes, implicitly, first-person plural (2010). Learning is like that. It can be third-
person – shaped and driven by a teacher or an examination syllabus – or it can be
first-person – arising from the social and emotional needs of individuals, but once the
learning has happened it becomes part of who 'we' are in the widest possible sense. What
students encounter in or because of the classroom experience thus becomes part of

themselves and by implication part of our collective understanding of who we are in relation to one another.

When we talk about the short story in a later book in this series about English, we use Horace's phrase *in medias res* – which means 'in the midst of things' to describe how we are often dropped into a story that is already under way. Effective learning is similarly a surprising, immediate and intense experience – and as a result we often (or *should* often) find ourselves not on the outside looking in, but in the middle of what we are learning. In recent times, for instance, particularly in the media, historians almost always recount the events of the past in the present tense. This is not affectation, but rather a recognition that the stories from history – just like those from science, or mathematics, or any school subject – exist in a perpetual 'now'.

All this leads us to our first principle: our students' need for a quality learning experience is **urgent and immediate**.

What do we mean by a 'quality learning experience'? When able students in a prominent independent school were asked this question they were less than complimentary about what they saw as their school's priorities: too much teaching to the requirements of examinations; too much reinforcement; too many practice papers; too much competition; a culture dominated by the fear of getting things wrong and, most of all, a pervasive cynicism about 'playing the game' – by which we suppose they meant, *means* (what they were given to learn) being entirely about the *ends* (the exam or the university interview) – an absence of tangents, a curtailing of curiosity and a focus on answers to the detriment of questions. What they really wanted, was the reverse: lots of tangents, curiosity driving motivation and an encouragement of questions.

When teachers (in another high achieving school) were asked the same question, their focus was not the same at all. Top of their list was how well or otherwise they understand and had found ways to apply the exact expectations of the examination syllabus. This for them would be what *urgency* and *immediacy* meant. This anxiety – and there is no other word for it – suggests that much of what happens in the classroom is not about 'now' but some future test. Much of what the teachers added to their list concerned their students' inability to handle criticism, their lack of resilience – and their impenetrability in general. So, the question for us in the classroom is how to make what we teach, 'present tense'; about immediate rather than deferred rewards for learning.

This brings us to a second principle: do we talk about and seek to provide a **dynamic** in our subject (and whole school, come to that) that is responsive, enabling and energetic? Has the examination syllabus – or political directives or league tables – become our default position? Is pretty well everything we do, and allow our students to do, measured in terms of relevance to some future moment of assessment? In *Originals: How Non-Conformists Change the World* (2016), Adam Grant talks about the difference between *déjà vu* and *vuja de*. *Déjà vu* experiences in the classroom would be when students meet all new learning experiences as though they have seen them before. This would explain those teacher criticisms about lacklustre students who cannot take criticism and are anything but resilient. *Vuja de* encounters in the classroom would be with familiar materials but approaching and responding to them in a new way. This is exactly what those independent school students mentioned earlier when they talked about what they really wanted from their learning experiences: more questioning, increased opportunities for independent thinking and an exposure to new options to discover the potential of a topic or a subject. As Adam Grant says, repeated opportunities to *question the default* (2016).

This is all a way of saying that the *dynamic* of a subject needs to be about its po[
breadth, its inherent opportunities for students to acquire knowledge, develop ι
standing and learn and practise skills, but even more, to do all these things in *exc[
ways; and by exceptional we mean *in ways that the teacher did not expect*. Once h‿‿‿‿
by the idea that a subject has its own dynamic, students become more independent, are
better able to work with concentration, have greater resilience and seek out new
opportunities for learning. We hope!

On to a third principle: an awareness that more able students, particularly those with
additional needs, require of us that we develop a **holistic** approach to their needs and
what we provide for them.

This means seeing their academic and aspirational needs alongside their social and
emotional well-being. Of course, this is to do with hearing and using their 'voice' as part
of the learning process – exactly what those independent school students were talking
about when they mentioned their need to break away from what they perceived as a
cynical utilitarian culture of focusing only on those elements of learning that are necessary
to reach the next stage.

The former high mistress of St Paul's independent school for girls, Clarissa Farr, says
that some parents, and by implication, some teachers, tend to 'snowplough' out of the
way any perceived obstacles in the path of what *they* imagine to be the road to perfection
– and those obstacles (or what adults might see as irrelevant issues) may be a student's
individual social and emotional needs. The pursuit of academic excellence is important,
of course, but only in the context of meeting the **holistic** needs of individual students
and not, necessarily, by meeting the needs of teachers, schools and parents. If Oxbridge
or Yale or Harvard is what a student chooses, then of course we do all we can to support
that ambition. The point is that it is a choice for the student, not the teachers or the
parent. 'Snowploughing' a student's views out of the way can only result in that students'
inability to manage and face future difficulties alone.

Mention of supporting academic ambition brings us to the fourth and final principle:
how **practical** is our support for students – along the road to whatever form of
perfection they have chosen? A recent and rather lack-lustre parliamentary speech was
described by an observer as being *all hat and no rabbit*. Our students need the hats –
practice, 'coaching', exam grades – the necessary thorough and focused grounding. They
also need the 'rabbits': exposure to bigger questions and ideas, conversations with experts,
a willingness to follow through on tangents, a reading culture that goes beyond the
expedient and allows students to 'question the default'. Learning that surprises!

In terms of the university interview, these things are much more than some rehashed
1960s idealism. They are entirely practical. University interviews focus on questions
rather than on given answers, on big ideas rather than isolated pieces of knowledge, on
reading more than set books, on how subject disciplines overlap rather than being
isolated in their own bubble. They are about *thinking* rather than *knowing*.

Which all brings us back to Graham Swift's phrase, *first-person plural*. Learning happens
not just when teachers teach, or when students repeat, rehearse or apply. It happens
when the teacher, or the book, the student and his or her peers come together to make
those fleeting moments in the lesson always there – in the present tense. First- and third-
person learning suggests a binary system – one or the other – success or failure – one
better, one worse. Then truth is that effective learning does not have its source in one

approach rather than the other. We are delivered to who we are because what we have learned has come from the recognising and braiding together of our collective voices and stories.

Despite the sometimes-oppressive emphasis on measuring performance and the *anxious literalism* (Bailey,2002) that envelopes some of us as a result, clues are there in much of the literature about how we might move forward and what accountability for our work should really mean. As early as 2003, Ofsted noted that for the most part, whole class *interactive teaching remains a one-way teacher-dominated activity. . . . In too many lessons teacher talk dominates and there are too few opportunities for pupils to talk and collaborate to enhance their learning.* As must be clear by now, we are accountable for more than test results. As we say repeatedly in this series of books, whatever subject specialism is laid out on the table for our dissection, what really marks us out as successful teachers is evidence that our students learn through **quality dialogue**, what Hymer *et al.* would call *the integration of prior knowledge with cognitive structures.* That influential advocate of meaningful conversations, Robert Fisher insists that: *'dialogue is the primary means or developing intelligence in the human species and problems in life and learning are primarily solved and our intelligence developed through dialogue with others'.*[5]

This is where all this is leading – away from circular arguments about what the more able are called and how we recognise them, towards a serious consideration of **how** we nurture, respond to and – even – create an environment where high achievement can flourish.

This question of **how** we make this happen will be addressed in other chapters and books in the series, but *for now* the answer to our question about why we do not seem to have taken to heart the demand that we pay more attention to the needs of the more able should be disentangled, for some of us, from some of the following thoughts:

1. Has the way the more able agenda encourages us to make judgements about ability caused us to *suspect* that agenda because it implies that ability is fixed and progress is linear?
2. Are we uncomfortable with the idea that ability needs to be identified sooner rather than later, and therefore fear closing the door on the possibility of transforming experiences *at any time* in a student's life?
3. How *sensitive and flexible* are we to those social, emotional, relational and motivational factors that might influence variations in student performance?
4. Does our approach in the classroom involve the co-construction of learning where students and teacher are co-participants – as Hymer, Fisher *et al.* advocate? How comfortably does this idea sit alongside what you see as the needs of your more able students, of your class and of your school?
5. Whose values are we teaching in our classrooms? The school's? Society's? The government's? Or – is it more a question of *modelling* values in the way that we teach, give feedback and the way we listen?
6. Does our work in the various subjects help students discover their own values?

Finally, how do we stimulate a curiosity to learn? In his work identifying the central importance of igniting and nurturing curiosity in schools, Erik Shonstrom (2013) makes the following observation:

Curiosity is inherently dynamic and propulsive, not sedentary and passive. Most traditional instruction depends on the latter state and seeks to control the former.

Which parts of these two sentences hold a mirror to our own classrooms and schools?

Notes

1. You will have noticed that this is a phrase we don't use in our discussions: it has passed its sell-by date as a phrase – but not as a concept, of course.
2. DfE: published 2011 for Primary Schools and 2012 for Secondary Schools in the UK.
3. At age 10/11 years.
4. Look at what we have to say about the Flynn Effect in the chapter on Intelligence; see also the Glossary.
5. Robert Fisher: *Teaching Thinking: Philosophical Enquiry in the Classroom*; Bloomsbury 2013. For practical approaches see also: Robert Fisher: *Creative Dialogue: Talk for Thinking in the Classroom*; Routledge 2009.

References

Bailey, Mary: 'What does research tell us about how we should be developing written composition?' In *Raising Standards in Literacy*; Fisher, Brooks and Lewis (eds); Oxford: Routledge Falmer 2002.

Eyre, Deborah: *What Really Works*; National Academy for Gifted and Talented Youth 2008.

Fisher, Robert: *Creative Dialogue: Talk for Thinking in the Classroom*; Oxford: Routledge 2009.

Fisher, Robert: *Teaching Thinking: Philosophical Enquiry in the Classroom*; London: Bloomsbury 2013.

Hymer, Whitehead and Huxtable: *Gifts, Talents and Education: A Living Theory Approach*; Hoboken, NJ: Wiley-Blackwell 2008.

Okri, B.: *TES*; 29th September 2000.

Rosen, Michael: *The Guardian*; September 2016.

Shonstrom, Eric: *Education Week*; June 2013.

Shonstrom, Eric: *Wild Curiosity: How to Unleash Creativity and Encourage Lifelong Wondering*; London, MD: Rowman and Littlefield Education 2015.

Sutton Trust, The: *Educating the Highly Able*; July 2012. Available at: www.suttontrust.com/research-paper/educating-the-highly-able-2/.

Swift, G.: 'Mothering Sunday'; *The Guardian* 2016.

Chapter 4

IQ and character
Boarding passes?

Intelligence is troublesome territory for teachers. As an abstract noun, even the word itself has become virtually meaningless in common usage, as common constructions and popular synonyms have combined to blur our understanding. The linguistic trough has also become corrupted through the word having been misguidedly linked to other words such as emotional, kinaesthetic, interpersonal and even naturalistic, that have little if any genuine association with cognitive ability. But perhaps most significantly, for many teachers the word has become a shorthand for Huxley's *Brave New World* style of pigeonholing of students based on the dangerous notions of heritability of intelligence and self-fulfilling prophecies.

Contrast this with the wide disparities in performance in many different fields being an accepted staple of human experience, as large permanent differences in individual talent are seen as part of natural human variation. As the commentator Akhandadi Das observed after the 2012 Olympics, sport itself is *a celebration of inequality* (2012) and it is assumed that elite athletes rely heavily on the genetic components and variations in DNA that make them taller, faster, stronger. That these differences are accepted as innate qualities of individuals is undeniable. But for some reason, inequalities in academic performance seem to carry significantly more stigma.

As a result, the idea of 'fixed' intelligence has become an increasingly impolite topic of conversation, perhaps more unpalatable because it focuses us on the function of education. Is there such a thing as a 'general intelligence', and if so, is it immune to change? If there is, and we cannot close the gap, are we condemned to accept such inequality? What is then the point of schools? If it is fixed, does that mean that it is a permanent brake on what any of our students are capable of achieving? Is the notion of inherited intelligence itself regarded as a millstone around educators' necks? Are our genetic differences essentially Fate, determining student outcomes? We need to remember that just because something might be regarded as objectionable does not in any real sense make it any less valid.

Intelligence as a construct can be defined as a general mental capability that, among other things, involves the ability to reason, plan, solve problems, think abstractly, comprehend complex ideas, learn quickly and learn from experience. It is not merely book-learning, a narrow academic skill, or test-taking smarts. Rather, it reflects a broader and deeper capability for comprehending our surroundings, 'making sense' of things, and figuring out what to do (Hauser, 2010). It is marked by high level cognition, motivation, and self-awareness. It is a cognitive process. It gives humans the abilities to learn, form concepts, understand, and reason, including the capacities to recognise patterns, comprehend ideas, plan, problem solve, and use language to communicate. Critically, there is a strong correlation between a wide range of different cognitive abilities, known as the 'positive manifold', which strongly supports the notion that there is an underlying general intelligence that is a fundamental property of the individual. None of this supports the idea of multiple intelligences, where any interest or ability can be redefined as 'intelligence', the theory and definitions of which have been thoroughly debunked by numerous researchers as tautologous and thus unfalsifiable (Baines, Adey, & Dillon, 2012). The finding that all mental tests positively inter-correlate is undeniable, that the scores reflect real differences in ability and the fact that these tests have a reliability *'higher than many medical tests'* as Andrew Sabisky adds, *'it is probably the most replicated result in all psychology'* (qtd. in Didau, 2015).

IQ tests predict academic achievement extremely well

Originally a test to measure intellectual skills, it was devised in 1904 by Alfred Binet to help teachers adapt their teaching to the needs of individual students. He defined intelligence as *judgement . . . good sense . . . the faculty of adapting to one's circumstances* and argued that it combined several skills all of which were shaped by a child's environment (Cherry, 2017). Binet's intention to promote personalised learning through his version of an IQ test was subsequently overshadowed by those who believed that intelligence was *not* in fact an overlapping collection of different skills and abilities, but rather a *fixed trait* – linked to genetics. What began with Binet's innocent quest to find the best way to teach individual children has been used to 'other' people, to segregate, diminish, undermine those individuals by using those tests to link intelligence with gender, race, nationality, class, background, or faith. Once that portion of the population has been 'othered' by a ruling elite, who has a say and who doesn't have a say is fixed. In schools, the notion of testing for intelligence (IQ) has come to be seen, by some, as part of that process of making some children eligible (or otherwise) for the glittering prizes. Once the label has been written, the concern is that it will last forever – leaving teachers wondering what they are supposed to be doing if decisions about how smart or otherwise a student is have already been made. Using a child's background to predict the future is a version of the same thing. We know what to expect. As teachers, we end up feeling 'a bit unnecessary' or even worse, part of some race- or class-driven stereotyping programme.

This process of 'othering' is suggested by Raymond Williams in his reflections on the word 'education' (1976). For him the pathways taken or not taken by a student are not to do with IQ, they are to do with where a child is born:

> To **educate** *was originally to rear or bring up children . . . but it has been specialised to (mean) organised teaching and instruction. . . . When a majority of children had no such organised instruction the distinction between educated and uneducated was reasonably clear, but, curiously, this distinction has been more common **since** the development of generally organised education and even of universal education.*

Williams' use of the word 'curiously' is heavily ironic. For him, it is not curious at all: it's about class. He concludes his brief definition of education with another moment of faux surprise:

It remains remarkable that after nearly a century of universal education in Britain the majority of the population should . . . be seen as uneducated or half-educated . . .

Why is this? Williams would say it's about how the 'level' of education experienced by a minority is continually adjusted to leave the majority of people who have received an education below that level. In other words, the way we define an 'educated' person alters to ensure that the haves and the have-nots remain in an unequal relationship. He would say that whether or not we succeed in education depends on the environment in which we are born and brought up. Or as Adolphe Quetelet put it, *society prepares the crimes and the guilty are the instrument by which it is executed* (1942). Williams would say that the fault, or limitation on how 'educated' we become, is not in ourselves, but in the home, the street, the school and the country we live in. Those academics who promote this view are known as *situation psychologists* – our culture and circumstances shape our behaviour and what we make of ourselves. Had he chosen to mention IQ scores, he would probably have said that they too are called into service to what Michael Rosen called, locking *millions of people* into a system dominated by *segregation and rejection* (2017), the main purpose of which is to make sure that some children don't *have to hang out with the oiks and the yobbos* (2016).

The Flynn effect

Having said all this, it might seem to some justifiable to dismiss IQ tests as suspect. Early in the twentieth century, in the UK, the educational psychologist Cyril Burt's work on IQ concluded that general intelligence was all about genetics and inheritance, and for schools he developed written tests for children that quantified verbal and non-verbal reasoning. The scores from these tests became an individual's Intelligence Quotient (IQ) (Robinson, 2011). Burt's pupil, Hans Eysenck, took this further in the 1960s, when he insisted that intelligence was all about inheritance and very little to do with environment. Acknowledging traits, in ourselves as well as others, seems to suggest that there are key aspects of our intelligence that are fixed and that whatever we do in the classroom cannot change who we or our students are, whatever we do. We can't but help thinking, too, that the sort of 'typing' trait theory encourages is likely to produce bigoted students – not only about people from other backgrounds, but as importantly, about themselves: I don't understand because I'm thick, I live in the wrong place, my parents are poor, I don't speak properly – and so and so on. If we believe that deep in the core of our being there are immovable 'traits' then, as teachers, our whole *raison d'etre* might well come crashing down.

James Flynn and what has come to be called the Flynn effect has come to our rescue as a more than convincing way of demolishing the link between IQ and gene pools. Flynn showed that IQ scores among racial minorities rose quite markedly over the period between 1910 and 1980 (1987). Gene pools could not have changed so dramatically over the same period. This does not mean there is no link between DNA and intelligence – quite the reverse, there is a good deal of current research to say that there is a very high, if quite complex, correlation[1] – simply that, like so much else of what we say here, there are other variables.

And yet . . . Taking such a righteous stance about IQ tests misses something. When Binet devised and promoted his system of testing for intelligence he lived in a world where receiving an education depended almost entirely on a child's socioeconomic background. For Binet, as for those who use such tests today – and despite Williams' fears about manipulated quotients – measuring intelligence irrespective of background is at least an attempt to level the playing field. More than that, there is overwhelming evidence that there is a correlation between both DNA and intelligence and between IQ and later examination results. It's too easy to persuade ourselves that IQ is not only irrelevant, it's also iniquitous, but it is a real and provable factor to consider alongside many others.

Yet what is interesting, and encouraging, about the work done by James Flynn and others is that it has been conclusively shown that measures of cognitive ability often increase over time. For this to happen surely they need to be highly motivated, independent learners with teachers who provide stimulating materials and a broad range of reading materials?[2]

What are the agreements within the research community experts?

'Mainstream Science on Intelligence' was a controversial public statement issued on 13 December 1994 by a group of academic researchers in fields associated with intelligence testing that presented those findings that were widely accepted in the expert community. The paper presented 25 conclusions, and they cover areas such as intelligence as a very general mental capability that reflects a broader and deeper capability for comprehending our surroundings. They believe that intelligence tests measure it well, as they are among the most accurate, reliable and valid of all psychological tests and assessments. Perhaps more controversially, the paper concludes that IQ is strongly related, probably more so than any other single measurable human trait, to many important educational, occupational, economic, and social outcomes and that whatever IQ tests measure, it is of great practical and social importance. It clearly states that while differences in intelligence are not the only factor affecting performance in education, training, and complex jobs, intelligence is often the most important.

So where does that leave us?

Questions about intelligence, how we as educators recognise it and what we do with that knowledge still haunt the ways we see and teach. Defining intelligence is only a start. Where does intelligence come from? Is intelligence inborn or is it malleable? Does measuring IQ and taking DNA into account correlate with academic achievement? Where does character and temperament *fit* into the picture? In part, these are questions about nature and/or nurture but the minute we frame them as binary oppositions, we are pulled up short with the thought that they may be inter-related. Which of course they are. The two sources of variation, genes and environment, are hopelessly compounded. Parents, for example, supply both. We are products of gene-environment interactions far too complex for any component analysis. Our environment changes how genes are expressed. Throw into the equation questions about how the toxic-stress (Tough, 2016) of a disadvantaged early life might disrupt cognitive development and we begin to see that finding a way to understand of all these questions so that we might become better teachers, particularly of more able students, is almost certain to make our heads hurt.

We sometimes choose to avoid these questions altogether either because of their dark historical echoes or a fear that we could fall into the discomfort of political incorrectness. That discomfort is there because although an understanding of intelligence began as a way to analyse the way individuals learn – and so teach them more effectively – it then seemed to develop as a way to *sort* children. What began as an educational aid, became a political tool. All those arguments about how or even whether we should identify the most able are an extreme version of the way what a child needs and what the 'system' needs can pull teachers in different directions.

The durable realities: Temperament and character?

The American, Francis Galton would argue that testing for intelligence, or worrying about class and social position are nowhere near as important as temperament and character – which he called, *durable realities, and persistent factors of our* conduct (1884). Success in education was to him about our temperament. It's in ourselves, who we are deep down, our personality. A glance back through the twentieth century will show just how enthusiastically this idea has been taken up. There are scores of personality- and trait-based assessments being used by employers – notably the Myers-Briggs Type Indicator (MBTI), which categorises personality into sixteen types, and the Enneagram test, which identifies nine. It became a huge industry, much like astrology.

Critics of these tests point out that those taking a personality test will tend to map their own personalities against the given categories or that the tests are blunt instruments, only identifying our most prominent traits.[3] Testing for traits is based on the belief that such tests can get to the very heart of who we are and can uncover our essential wiring, which once exposed will predict exactly how we are likely to perform in any given situation.

This is called *essentialist thinking* and it is both a *cause and a consequence of typing* (Rose, 2015). Todd Rose argues, quite vehemently, that in practice, '*personality traits explain no more than nine percent of behaviour*'[4] and yet tests such as these are used as part of employers' selection procedures. It's difficult to avoid the conclusion that such tests, rather than revealing an individual's potential are simply a means of rationing scarce resources. In the world or work, the scarce resources are the number of jobs available, in schools it's the number of places available at one type of school or another – or a way of ensuring that the schools and teachers who prepare their pupils best for these tests remain the exception rather than the rule. There's a sort of hopelessness about trait theory.

This is not to say that something like traits or characteristics do not exist – except the word 'inclinations' rather than traits might pack less baggage. How else do you explain a child who is naturally funny – has 'funny bones' – or a Charles Darwin type who loves collecting and labelling – or any number of children who are *inclined* towards writing or reading, or maths, or craft or music or sport? We don't look at these children in our classrooms and talk about them as having an *essential nature*. If we did that we would miss other, equally important, aspects of their personality. We can have 'inclinations' but do not have to be defined by them.

The truth is, the way people behave depends on who they are *and* the situation they are in. This **context principle**, *asserts that individual behaviour cannot be explained or predicted apart from a situation, and the influence of a situation cannot be specified without reference to the individual experiencing it.*[5]

The importance of this combination of traits and situation has led to a notion known as '*if-then signatures*' (Kammrah, 2005), which is about addressing issues of behaviour or performance by examining the context in which that behaviour or performance takes place. For instance, a student may be successful in a classroom where there is dialogue and debate, and unsuccessful in a situation where dialogue is discouraged. For another student, the conditions for success may be the reverse.

In the UK there was, in the early part of this century, a drive towards defining what sort of classroom 'situation' best provided for an effective climate for learning – a climate where, perhaps, if-then signatures could be accommodated in appropriate permutations. The key elements in this initiative were to identify strategies that would encourage: high expectations; engagement and responsibility; students working beyond the functional and finding ways to 'share the struggle' – all within a context of what was then called 'personalised learning'. Perhaps the more recent word, *equifinality*, might offer an alternative way of describing this process.[6] It means that there are a whole number of ways to achieve knowledge and understanding – there are *always* alternative routes to get from one place to another.

Not recognising equifinality is just, if not more, likely to happen when there is a lack of challenge in what we offer to students rather than when we demand too much. With the most able, we may fear burnout when the real problem is lack of ignition: because our aspirations for our students are bounded by what is, for some students, a limited horizon, we fail to explore those alternative routes to learning which might better inspire. An over-reliance on identifying traits to define the exact nature of provision in the classroom is just as likely to lead to an atrophy of potential as it is to its fulfilment.

The shift away from nature towards nurture has led, perhaps, to the packing of airport bookshop shelves with books telling us that our brains are not 'hardwired' for either success or failure, but are in fact more than anything, quite 'plastic'. Willpower is the key; we can create outcomes in our lives through how we use our minds. Mastery, say these books, is within reach if you *believe* it is within reach. Robert Greene, for instance, argues that *social and political barriers have mostly disappeared* and as a result, we are all closer than we think to becoming geniuses (2012).

Perhaps we can hear the ghost of Raymond Williams banging at the door?

Lou Adler applied context-focused thinking to the workplace (2012). Instead of attempting to define what sort of *person* a company might need, he set about defining the *job* they wanted done. Applied to schools this would mean, for instance, you might hope that promising student scientists would be inquisitive about how and why things work. Being inquisitive with the teacher, with peers and with parents might require different approaches and skills: with the teacher, it would involve the confidence to listen and question; with peers, the sort of inter-personal skills that encourage off-piste interests and activities, and with parents (and older members of the family) an openness to mining their past experiences. Adler would argue that there is no such thing as an all-round inquisitive person. What that teacher, those peer group members and that family wanted from this budding scientist, and might respond to, was inquisitiveness in different contexts.

What this adds up to for teachers is that they need to think through what Adler calls, *the contextual details of the job* and as a result *not* to ask questions such as, why is this student underperforming, but rather, why is this student underperforming *in this context*? Asking that first question comes from only seeing that student in just one context. One or two personality traits in a single context will tell us very little about a student – or anyone else, for that matter.

So where does this leave us? Given that we are teachers, what we need is *learnable skills* not immovable hardwiring. We might accept that inclinations rather than traits have some part to play in the learning process, and we probably agree that a keen awareness of the context or climate for learning has an important part to play. Similarly, it is probably the case as we said earlier when we used the word equifinality, that we have come to question what has been called *normative thinking* – the idea that there is only one *normal* way to learn – and to allow for and embrace – cautiously, given the average teacher's workload – the concept of *equifinality* – those possibilities offered by multidimensional interactions between the student and what they are required, or want, to learn.

A last thought, before we move on to discuss what we hope will be more learnable skills. It's the issue of *pace*. Perhaps it's a result of all those reality shows where contestants have complicated tasks (or cakes) to complete in very limited time, but we have come to see going faster as better. Speed denotes high ability. Faster equals smarter. It's not a new idea: Edward Thorndike wrote in 1908 (in *The Human Nature Club*) that, *it is the quick learners who are the good retainers*. Todd Rose (2015) objects to this idea and concludes that:

> by demanding that our students learn at one fixed pace, we are artificially impairing the ability of many to learn and succeed . . . The architecture of our education system is simply not designed to accommodate such individuality, and it therefore fails to nurture the potential and talent of all its students.

Quoting research by Kurt Fischer of Harvard, Rose goes on to promote the idea of *individual pathways* – of thinking of learning, not as a ladder but as a *web of development*.

Two skills. Academics and character

This subtitle is taken from a KIPP (Knowledge is Power Program) t-shirt: being smart at *academic* work is good but having a smart *character* or personality is just as good. We have to say, before we embark on some thoughts about how teaching character (resilience and conscientiousness, for instance) might be the solution to worries about maximising achievement, that there is a huge danger of allowing ourselves to slip into one-dimensional thinking. This chapter is bursting with examples of people who thought they had the 'answer', the magic bullet that would make the way their students learn and are taught the envy of the world. Individuals are more complex than that: Todd Rose calls this complexity the *jaggedness principle* which means, in essence, that coming up with a one-dimensional solution to a multi-dimensional problem is a lost cause. Relying on a small set of familiar metrics, such as IQ or personality tests, or a measure of deprivation (such as eligibility for free school meals) can lead to an underestimation of a child's complex capacities and needs. Picking and mixing approaches to teaching and learning would almost certainly make more sense, which is probably what teachers do all the time, but books in search of the 'big idea', do not.

A writer who is more balanced than most, Paul Tough, dismisses the idea that character and traits are the same thing and as a result are unchanging. He defines character as: *a set of abilities or strengths that are very much changeable – entirely malleable, in fact. They are skills you can learn; they are skills you can practice; and they are skills you can teach* (2012). To illustrate his point, he tells the story of the KIPP movement, which mushroomed across the USA from the 1990s. The intention of this movement was to transform underperforming, disadvantaged students into scholars on their way to college. The strategy was immersive, high-intensity teaching and learning coupled with an overt attention to attitude and learning behaviour. The test scores from the first schools caused a sensation and the movement rapidly attracted funding to expand to over a hundred charter schools country-wide. However, as those first progressed onto college courses, the drop-out rate was unacceptably high. The students thrived in the paternalistic school environment and faltered away from it. Perhaps, KIPP leaders thought, character development had been neglected. They hadn't ignored character and were, in the early days, very much influenced by Martin Seligman's book, *Learned Optimism* (1991), and had recognised the importance of understanding 'the science of character' but had not gone far enough. The next stage quantified seven desirable character strengths: grit, self-control, zest, social intelligence, gratitude, optimism and curiosity. Angela Duckworth joined the project and articulated the importance of character under two distinct headings: the ways it drives motivation and its importance as a generator of the volition – that is, willpower and self-control. In her later book, she repeats what she sees as the two overarching contributions made to learning and achievement by character:

> [N]o matter the domain, the highly successful had a kind of ferocious determination that played out in two ways. First, these exemplars were unusually resilient and hard-working. Second, they knew in a very, very deep way what it was they wanted. They not only had **determination**, they had **direction**.
>
> (2016)

The centrality Duckworth gives to these two aspects of character is reassuring to those who lean towards nurture – not *opposed* to nature, but as well as. The DNA does matter, so too does birth and circumstance, but what Duckworth calls *the function of experience* also matters – crucially, she would say. There are *no genes for grit*. Tough takes it further when he says that character can act as a safety net for those students who have limited support from their families and surrounding culture, or who stand a greater chance of making wrong turnings and choices. Without the safety net of class, *you need more grit, more social intelligence, more self-control than wealthier kids* (2015).

If, as we seem to be suggesting, character is malleable rather than fixed, can the same be said of intelligence? Carol Dweck would say so – or at least she would say that 'mindset' is (2017). The idea at the centre of Dweck's theory is powerful: if students believe they can 'grow' their intelligence and achieve more, rather than settle for an immovable ceiling on their potential, then (and research to some extent shows this) outcomes improve.[7] Although grit pales into insignificance when measured against the impact of IQ (0.18 correlation with academic achievement as opposed to 0.81).

When it comes to thinking about **how** we can 'teach' a growth mindset – develop intelligence and character – Duckworth would say it's a matter of focusing on both motivation and volition at the same time. Wall-to-wall 'positive fantasising' as Duckworth calls it (about achieving your dreams of being rich and famous) are useless unless you can address the obstacles that make that ambition difficult. Duckworth and others have described what they call *mental contrasting* which invites the student to think about the positive outcomes from their endeavours and contrast those thoughts against the obstacles that will make that achievement tricky (Duckworth, Kirby, Oettingen and Gollwitzer, 2009). Matthew Syed talks about the importance of '*redefining failure*' if we are to achieve high performance (2015). For Duckworth and others, it is entirely feasible for us and our students to see 'character' and 'intelligence' as habits of mind and of behaviour. They both have an essential default position: conscientiousness.

Non-cognitive qualities, character and personality, are now taken seriously as key factors in educational achievement. Conscientiousness, persistence, self-discipline and Duckworth's 'grit' – and the way she highlights how important it is to be able to deal with failure – are all crucial. For Duckworth, developing character, or 'grit' comes down to the concept of *follow-through*. This is about sticking with a goal over an extended period, about continuous commitment. A child or student's capacity to *practice grit* perhaps best finds expression in extracurricular activities. Duckworth reasons that children are often drawn to such activities out of interest, and that when the adult in charge gets it right they are an effective mix of support and challenge. As a result, the child experiences purpose, ambition, hope and the rewards of practice. It's a powerful combination of approaches: motivation and challenge, and the end product is the development of an individual's ability or character quality that enables them to follow-through on a commitment. Providing or challenging young people with such activities not only invites the use of what Duckworth calls, 'grit' but also builds that quality.

Which all brings us back to where this chapter began: with Raymond Williams and his conviction that class is a key player, and Paul Tough with his contention that character is a powerful 'safety net' which can protect children against the inequalities of their culture and society. Tough, like Dweck, would argue that the way we *teach* and interact with our students can play a vital part in shaping character. Duckworth would not disagree, but would add that extracurricular activities are a particularly effective way to develop those qualities that lead to the 'glittering prizes'. Quoting Harvard political scientist, Robert Putnam, she adds as a warning against complacency that in recent times there has been a widening gap in extracurricular participation between rich and poor. Raymond Williams is still banging on the door, tapping on the window.

Angela Duckworth concludes her discussion of 'grit' with a strategy she uses in her own family: the 'hard thing rule'. It has three parts: everyone in the family or the class, including the teacher, chooses 'a hard thing' which they will need regular practice to achieve: the time scale is proposed and agreed; dropping out is not allowed other than at agreed points – like such as the end of the season, or when the subscription runs out; the 'hard thing' is entirely the choice of the individual.

Is teaching worthwhile?

The development of character happens mostly when students are encouraged to persevere through encounters with challenging academic work. Qualities such as resilience, grit, follow-through are attractive ideas but there is little hard evidence that they are all that *teachable*, or that they make a lasting difference when it comes to achievement – but Tough, after promoting character education enthusiastically, comes to doubt whether it can in fact be taught directly. At best, he thinks, developing character as an outcome of classroom challenge is a powerful safety-net for students in an uncertain world (2015). Elsewhere we mention Adam Grant's notion of *déjà vu* versus *vuja de*. Relying on IQ scores and socioeconomic and family information leads us to see what we expect to see. Such knowledge and expectations are a default position, an emotional painkiller which prevents us from being dissatisfied with the way things are. If nothing else, James Flynn's discoveries about how intelligence alters over time, should warn us against a 'we have been here before' perspective in schools. We probably shouldn't expect to radically alter the real individual differences in academic achievement overnight, but we can certainly increase the knowledge base that is in our schools and create a better educated society overall. Grant's *vuja de* is a more realistic and potentially rewarding way to see our work; looking with a new perspective invites fresh solutions to old problems.

Notes

1. See Plomin, Robert: *Genetics and Intelligence*, and Dreary *et al.*: *Intelligence and Educational Achievement*; 2006. See also press reports on Dr Michael Johnson of Imperial College London and his research on the link between genes and intelligence.
2. See studies by Echols *et al.* 1996; Sameoff *et al.* 1993; Stanovich *et al.* 1995.
3. For example: Baer, Drake: 'Why the Meyers-Briggs Personality Test is Misleading, Inaccurate and Unscientific'; *Business Insider* 2014 and Cunningham, Lilian: 'Myers-Briggs: Does it Pay to Know Your Type'; *Washington Post* 2012.
4. He uses a whole library of evidence for this, most prominently Noftle and Robins (2007); Holland and Glenn (2008); Mischel (2013).
5. This is Todd Rose's summary of Yuichi Shoda's finding in *The Person in Context: Building a Science of the Individual*; Guilford Press 2007.
6. Several papers exploring equifinality: Cicchetti and Rogosch (1996); Schneider and Somers (2006) and Keith Bevan (2006).
7. See Kristin Line Froedge on applying Dweck's theories: 'The Effect of a Growth Mindset on Student Achievement Among Students with a Disability'[Diss] Western Kentucky University, 2017.

References

Adler, Lou: *Hire with Your Head: Using Performance-Based Hiring to Build Great Teams*; Hoboken, NJ: John Wiley and Sons 2012.

Baines, E., Adey, P. and Dillon, J. (eds): *Bad Education: Debunking Myths in Education – From fixed IQ to multiple intelligences*; Oxford: Oxford University Press 2012.

Baer, Drake: 'Why the Meyers-Briggs Personality Test is Misleading, Inaccurate and Unscientific'; *Business Insider* 2014.

Cherry, K.: 'Alfred Binet & the History of IQ Testing: The Development of Modern Intelligence Quotient Testing' 2017. Available at: www.verywell.com/history-of-intelligence-testing-2795581.

Cunningham, Lilian: 'Myers-Briggs: Does it Pay to Know Your Type'; *Washington Post* 2012.

Das, Akhandadi: 'Thought for the Day' 5 September, 2012. Retrieved from www.bbc.co.uk/programmes/p00y88ml.

Didau, David: *What If Everything You Know About Education Is Wrong?* Carmathen, UK: Crown House Publishing, June 2015.

Deary, Strand, Smith, Fernandes: 'Intelligence and Educational Achievement'; *Intelligence, 35,* 2007. pp. 13–21.

Duckworth, Angela: *Grit: The Power of Passion and Perseverance*; London: Vermilion 2016.

Duckworth, Kirby, Oettingen and Gollwitzer: 'Mental Contrasting', *Journal of Applied Developmental Psychology*, 2009.

Dweck, Carol: *Mindset: Changing the Way You Think*; London: Robinson (Updated) 2017.

Flynn, J.R.: 'Massive IQ gains in 14 nations: what IQ tests really measure'; *Psychological Bulletin* 1987.

Froedge, K.L.: 'The Effect of a Growth Mindset on Student Achievement Among Students with a Disability'[Diss], Bowling Green, KY: Western Kentucky University, 2017.

Galton, Francis: 'Measurement of Character'; *Fortnightly Review, 42,* 1884.

Greene, Robert: *Mastery*; London: Profile Books 2012.

Hauser, Robert M.: 'Causes and Consequences of Cognitive Functioning Across the Life Course'; *Educational Researcher*, 9, 2010.

Kammrath, L.K., Mendoza-Denton, R., Mischel, W.: 'Incorporating if-then Personality Signatures in person Perception: Beyond the Person-Situation Dichotomy'; *Journal of Personality and Social Psychology*, 88, 2005.

Plomin, Robert: 'Genetics and Intelligence' *Talent Development III*, 1995. pp. 19-39.

Quetelet, Adolphe: *Sur l'homme*; 1942. Available at: www.oxfordjournals.org/our_journals/ndtplus/.

Robinson, A.: 'Sudden Genius', 2011. Available at: www.psychologytoday.com/blog/sudden-genius/201101/is-high-intelligence.

Rose, Todd: *The End of Average: How to Succeed in a World that Values Sameness*; London: Penguin 2015.

Rosen, Michael: *The Guardian*; October 2016.

Rosen, Michael: *The Guardian*; May 2017.

Shoda, Yuichi: *The Person in Context: Building a Science of the Individual*; New York: Guilford Press 2007.

Syed, Matthew: *Black Box Thinking*; London: John Murray 2015.

Tough, Paul: *How Children Succeed: Grit, Curiosity and the Hidden Power of Character*; London: Random House 2012.

Tough, Paul: 'How Kids Learn Resilience'; *The Atlantic* 2016.

Williams, Raymond: *Keywords: A Vocabulary of Culture and Society*; Waukegan, IL: Fontana Press 1976.

Chapter 5

Submerged populations and overlooked student groups
Missing passengers?

Conceptual incoherence?

More able education is unavoidably tied to cultural concepts of excellence, and these ideas tend to reflect the society in which individuals live. What is prized in one culture may not be valued in another, and it is difficult to impose one belief system on a culture that may define talents very differently. A key task is to highlight the ways in which celebrating talents can lead to increased motivation in other areas of learning, wider educational achievement and transferable skills. A further task is to work with community groups in identifying and celebrating culturally relevant and appropriate talents.

Measures put into place in many countries worldwide to support students 'at risk' or 'hard to reach' tend not to focus much attention on the more able. It's as if these groups are regarded as somehow mutually exclusive. More able learners are of course not a homogenous group. They come from all backgrounds and have a wide range of abilities and talents. Teachers have a responsibility actively to seek potential in all students, and school assessment systems need to be rigorous and effective at all levels in order to identify individuals and groups of pupils who are at risk of underachievement, and to track the impact of interventions.

> *The pursuit of excellence has got absolutely nothing to do with elitism but it has everything to do with equality of opportunity. . . . The discoveries, the theories, the products, the techniques that will shape the nation's future will come about as a result of gifted individuals being prepared to take risks to push themselves to the limit in the search for excellence.*
>
> (Lord Puttnam of Queensgate, 2000)

The under-representation of, for example, minority ethnic children in 'gifted' education programmes in both the United Kingdom and the United States is well documented (Ball, 2013). Unfortunately, the issues are often misrepresented as simply the impact of disadvantage. As we shall explore, the reality is far more complex.

This is a core issue that needs to be faced within more able education generally. There are perhaps some inherent problems that need investigation. Does more able education actually have embedded in it the basis for the under-representation of certain groups outside the mainstream of any culture in which the concept is employed? Are the goals of able education and equity mutually exclusive? Does the practice of focusing on the more able in a multi-cultural society in which there are vast discrepancies in status simply serve to increase the gap between White and minority families?

Who is missed out and why?

Data suggests that significant numbers of pupils are not identified as gifted and talented because, for various reasons, their abilities are not recognised and nurtured (Gillborn, 2008). Particular groups of students who are vulnerable include those:

- with English as an additional language (EAL), including advanced bilingual pupils;
- who are from black and minority ethnic (BME) groups with a record of under-performance (including Black Caribbean, Pakistani, Bangladeshi, some mixed heritage, Gypsy Roma Traveller);
- children in care (looked after children);
- in small rural or isolated schools with limited resources.

Many of the most able student are drawn from communities with distinct social and cultural pressures. Special attention must be paid to those from these traditionally under-represented groups. This is achieved in part by working through the school system to improve the general education offer. However, each school must also use data to identify individual students from such groups and intervene to offer them access to the high-quality opportunities and the support they require to realise their potential.

> We need to create an educational system that sees equality as an essential requirement of effective more able education provision. Where all educators hold high expectations towards their culturally diverse students. Where schools celebrate the diversity, which is their strength. Where there is a requirement to be completely committed to breaking down the barriers that prevent individuals from realising their potential. Where high levels of challenge are the right of all students.

(REAL Project)

This statement of intent was written by the London Gifted & Talented team working on the REAL Project (see below). But it could equally have been written by them on the BME Project that they devised and wrote with the National Strategies or the Rural and Isolated guidance that they wrote for the DfE.[1] This chapter will look at each of the above groups in turn and explore some of the issues that have arisen. Teachers need to be open-minded about who can excel, avoid constructing 'glass ceilings' and understand that high achievement may only emerge when the appropriate opportunities are provided. A learner may have a predisposition to excel in one or more areas, but only demonstrate this if encouraged and supported to do so.

1. English as an additional language

LG&T ran a national academic literacy project over a 4-year period that engaged with 50 local education authorities and almost 1,500 schools. It was a project to improve the quality of more able education as part of a supported intervention to engage with the 'narrowing the gap' agenda through the use of more able strategies with an iden-tified target group of learners who have potential but are identified as being at risk of underachievement. A detailed analysis of potential vs. current achievement and standards was undertaken to build a positive picture of learner needs through an understanding of what success looks like for 'similar' learners. Its key focus was on academic literacy to increase standards and prove impact in formal test environments.

Who are advanced bilingual learners?

More able learners who are also advanced learners of English may be assumed to be self-sufficient, but often need additional support to master the demands of language or cultural references in order to achieve at the highest levels. An advanced bilingual learner is often an able student who sounds fluent, sounds probably like a native speaker of English. Due to their ability, they have often made impressive progress and their writing is quite good. But when looked at more closely, there are a number of features of it that show that English isn't their first language, and that they may be a long way short of the kind of academic language that they need. They won't acquire that by osmosis. They will only acquire it if we teach it to them explicitly. Formal English can be regarded as an additional language for many such students.

The learning needs of advanced learners are complex; there is no single set of barriers to learning that apply to all. They may be recent arrivals who have been educated in English language environments, or have been in school in England for several years. English may be their first language but they may use another at home. Some of the core features of this group that were captured in the project:

1. They tend to have more gaps in their academic vocabulary and handle certain features of writing less confidently for academic purposes than their peers with English as their mother tongue language (EMT).
2. They may have less grasp of idiomatic speech, or take things more literally than intended.
3. They may lack cultural capital – the understanding and exposure to the diversity of history, society and experience which are critical to high achievement.
4. They may be unfamiliar with the conventions and expectations of academic writing, such as how a scientific report differs from a summary of a historical event.
5. They may have good 'playground' English but this quality and confidence in social talk may not be mirrored in their ability to use formal language and genre.
6. They may slip into a more informal tone for a particular task when what is required is more formal language.
7. They may have good topic-level knowledge, but limited capacity to show what they know when answering questions. In other words, they may be topic-specific in answers rather than being question-specific, or write answers that read like lists.

What does high challenge teaching and learning look like for advanced learners?

Providing high challenge learning for EAL students depends on understanding how their learning needs might be meaningfully different from their peers. All learners, regardless of background are different. Meaningful differences are those that we need to focus on in order to differentiate learning. In a nutshell this means thinking about how the balance between challenge and support for advanced learners *may* need to be different to that for any other able learner. The key questions are, how do we provide differentiated support so that EAL learners can access challenge in normal classroom learning and what should be different about the learning opportunities we offer to build on their strengths?

The REAL Projects have identified five distinct areas on which classroom practice can be differentiated to meet the needs of more advanced learners.

* **A**nalysing questions and task requirements.
* **B**eing explicit about using English as a resource for learning.
* **H**ighlighting how language is used in particular contexts.
* **E**ncouraging pupils to think about the ways in which they can develop effective language learning strategies.
* **M**aking cultural references accessible.

There are significant differences between informal speech and formal written communication that many of our most able students who come from EAL backgrounds have little direct knowledge of, and little chance to acquire. Gaps in academic vocabulary often remain hidden due to apparent fluency in spoken English; without a good range of academic language many learners cannot achieve top grades and the vast majority will underachieve at some point.

What works to support language acquisition in advanced learners?

Language acquisition needs to be a structured process – which learners can then be taught how to do for themselves. The ability to understand and use academic language with precision can make a huge difference to the chances of achieving a top grade, as it is easy to lose marks in tests when students lack a precise understanding of meaning. If they are not precise, examiners are instructed to infer how much we know or understand, which for them, is partly an educated guess. The more accurate they are, the less is left to chance. Some of the most effective approaches are listed below;

* Use more formal talk as a bridge to writing.
* Ensure that learners have the opportunity to formally verbalise something which they are later going to write.
* Show the cultural context and extend the cultural reach of advanced learners to references which might be outside their experience.
* Make explicit the use and meaning of idiomatic expression and help pupils to become aware of idioms in particular contexts and to identify the difference between literal and figurative meaning.
* Use key visuals and model and use visual planning tools to support language development.
* Be explicit about grammar and give advanced learners the technical skills to achieve high grades in specialist subjects.
* Model sentences and give pupils a pattern for sentences which they can repeat with slight modifications.
* Spot technical and specialist vocabulary and pinpoint words that have a specific use in context, but also a common use. Isolate words rarely encountered beyond the subject (technical vocabulary).
* Collect and structure knowledge of vocabulary.

If we are not explicitly using these strategies, or focused on teaching these differences and the key command words in questions, it is highly unlikely that such students will just assimilate them from their home background or from the playground. We cannot always guess meanings from context when many words are missing, and with academic and subject language, guessing incorrectly can have serious consequences.

2. More able black and minority ethnic students

Within any cultural context, no one set of descriptions or prescriptions will suffice for all students from any background. As practitioners we must found our practice on the acknowledgement that individuals of similar cultural backgrounds may share attributes but are also unique – that each individual's 'portion' of a culture differs from that of any other individual. Many argue that it is important to recognise that there may be as much variation within any cultural group as there is between culture groups. Some Black learners are clearly under-performing, but there are Black learners who are highly successful. Others argue that there are some characteristics that are common to all Black pupils and that is why we need to interrogate what the data is telling us.

Recent research has also done a good job of pinpointing educational vulnerability. We need to destroy stereotypes and myths about the educational needs of culturally-diverse students and lay a new foundation upon which to launch more useful practice.

What does research suggest about minority cultural underachievement?

Like all students, Black learners have a range of identities which unite to make them individual. Being able is just one. It is vital that schools recognise and acknowledge these multiple identities and break the cycle of cultural stereotyping of Black pupils and their parents which can impact negatively on relationships, expectations, and ultimately attainment. Very able underachieving students are highly conscious of the social constraints imposed by the environments in which they live, even if schools are substantially less aware.

International perspectives[2]

Many reasons have been researched regarding the underachievement of very able students from minority groups in the United States and the UK. What follows are summaries of key findings from research which may offer some insights into current thinking. It is only after we recognise potential that we can assess whether performance is below potential.

Minority students who do not believe in the achievement ideology, or who believe that glass ceilings and injustices will hinder their achievement, are not likely to work to their potential in school. This external locus of control attitude hinders minority students' achievements, as students who attribute their outcomes to external factors, such as discrimination, may put forth less effort than those who attribute outcomes to internal factors, such as effort and ability (Ford, 1996). In addition, low teacher expectations for minority students may relate to a lack of teacher training in both multicultural and more able education, and such unprepared teachers are less likely to refer minority students for more able education services. When students do not have access to appropriate education, they have difficulty reaching their potential, which may result in under-achievement due to disinterest, frustration and lack of challenge (Michelson 1984, 1990). These ideas are explained in more detail below.

Most Black students, according to Ford and Thomas (1997) must simultaneously manipulate two cultures; one at home and the other at school that may be quite diverse and the value conflict set up may affect their sense of self-worth.

Another widely-held supposition is that many Black children hide their academic abilities by becoming class clowns, dropping out, and suppressing effort to avoid being perceived as 'acting white', or otherwise rejecting or 'selling out' Black culture. Ford and Ogbu argue that school learning is consciously or unconsciously perceived as a subtractive process: a minority person who learns successfully in school or who follows the standard practices of the school is perceived as '*becoming acculturated into the white frame of reference at the expense of the minorities cultural frame of reference and collective welfare*' highlighting a choice between their need for achievement and their need for affiliation (1986).

The problem of more able students who lack motivation to participate in school or to strive to excel academically may simply reflect a mismatch between the child's motivational characteristics and the opportunities provided in the classroom. Therefore, more able students who are not challenged in school demonstrate both integrity and courage when they refuse to do the required work that is below them intellectually and are effectively '*dropping out with dignity*' (Reis, 1998).

Cultural capitalism

According to some social-structural explanations for school failure, poor academic performance among bright disadvantaged students is a result of the social stratification, marginality, and racism experienced by socially and culturally distinct individuals in the society at large. Inequalities in the social and educational systems therefore lead many disadvantaged individuals '*to reject academic competition and to perceive adaptation to the existing social structures as futile*' (Ogbu, 1978).

Assumptions of cultural deprivation based of difference

What is clear from the above research is that an able student's cultural background and frames of reference can force choices between the need for achievement and affiliation. This is not only a 'minority' issue. Schools will know their pupils' heritage, cultures, histories, experiences and needs. The picture is complex and pupils often juggle numerous identities in their everyday lives, switching from one to the other as necessity dictates. It is vital that schools recognise and acknowledge these multiple identities and break the cycle of cultural stereotyping of pupils and their communities that can impact negatively on relationships, expectations, and ultimately attainment. Claude Steele and Joshua Aronson pioneered 'stereotype threat' which shows that people's performances on many measures are automatically affected by their belief that they are doing something their 'group' is stereotypically good or bad at. They found that merely reminding people of a negative group stereotype worsens their performance.

The idea of meaningful difference is key to making personalisation manageable. Every more able learner is potentially affected by a range of characteristics which may have a particular effect on their learning. The combination of these factors tends to reflect how we relate to these individuals as learners and shapes the working assumptions on which planning is based.

It's impossible for educators to gain complete knowledge of the student groups they encounter, and the knowledge they acquire tends to be laden with stereotypes – often assuming cultural deprivation because of difference. A better focus is to look at the intersection of school and family/community contexts rather than on understanding the differences among ethnic cultures; those schools effective at raising Black attainment develop systemic strategies to get to know who their Black pupils are. Without this understanding, descriptively useful indicators begin to take on explanatory values, which can be extremely damaging.

The continuing underperformance of some groups of Black pupils is of concern. However, it must also be noted that this pattern is not uniform: in some schools, these learners attain at the highest levels. There has been considerable attention paid to issues of under-performance among Black student groups at baseline or floor target levels. What has not been so clearly analysed and therefore understood are the patterns of attainment and achievement at the highest levels.

Labelling and diversity

Framing all of this is the need to ensure a positive school climate, which includes high staff expectations, a demand for high academic performance, and a denial of the cultural deprivation arguments and stereotypes that support it. As the population continues to diversify – and 'Black students' fails to even begin to fully portray the stunning diversity among the populations it labels – so schools must adapt to and reflect this demographic transformation. The next generations of 'minority' students will continue to be vulnerable if our schools don't successfully complete the necessary metamorphosis. There must be clarity throughout our behaviours and actions so that schools can simultaneously recognise a student's background culture and those characteristics that define their uniqueness.

3. Rural and isolated

What is the impact of cultural influences on schools?

Able learners who live and/or attend schools in rural environments are a significant 'submerged' population whose needs are largely invisible and unconsidered, and for whom negative community-led expectations can have a severe impact on their attainment. Relatively few schools explicitly consider representation of rural learners as a sub-group of their identified more able population. This may be because many do not see rurality as a significant separate issue, or as a characteristic that is likely to affect achievement.

However, research by and on behalf of the National Rural Network (2010) indicates that schools do recognise that more able rural learners may have fewer opportunities for enrichment activities or specialist expertise, and more limited chances for peer working or access to Higher Education. Logistical and economic factors can also reduce the range and depth of choices available. Rural learners can have significantly reduced access to cultural diversity and experience. They may also compare themselves unfavourably to urban peers who they can consider to have broader life experience and more far-reaching aspirations. Traditions, insularity and inertia in some rural communities can also result in reluctance on the part of some parents and the community to support the school in promoting the wider interests and ambitions of children and young people, particularly when these are not seen to be compatible with their own community's survival. Small school provision, often in classes of mixed Key Stages, can make classroom differentiation a more challenging task for the classroom teacher. Budgetary constraints may lead to reduced access to ICT in small schools, compounded by a lack of availability of high speed internet. Teachers may have fewer opportunities for professional development due to transport, distance and cover issues. Headteachers with teaching workloads have less capacity to plan with, monitor and support colleagues. Rurality clearly is not a single issue, but one that interacts with others that combined may affect the range of opportunities, aspirations and access of rural learners to sustained engagement with the high challenge that in turn brings high achievement.

Communities exert huge power, and like all power it can be used for negative as well as positive ends. It is essential for schools to feel confident enough to challenge the local community where necessary to counter negative effects of insularity and lack of ambition, values conflict and lack of interest. In some communities in rural and isolated areas, it must be recognised that more able students can actually be held back, consciously or unconsciously, as success can be seen as a threat to the continued existence of that community. If a child goes off to a top university, is it likely that they will return? There is however a clear distinction that needs to be made between more affluent and stable rural communities and those for which the current climate is one of anxiety due to rapid economic change, as traditional forms of rural employment come under threat, vital services close or relocate, and younger people are forced to move to urban areas. For some, low income, poor housing, inadequate services and limited transport characterise day-to-day living in the countryside.

Although it is important to recognise that schools are not the only determinant of a learner's progress and that societal, cultural and personal factors all impact on how they will progress at school, schools need to address the many factors they have the power to control. Headteachers and senior leaders must have the courage and conviction to tackle challenging and controversial cultural factors and to facilitate open debate and understanding.

What can schools do to better engage with communities?

In outstanding schools, parental and community engagement often enhances and extends learning substantially beyond the taught curriculum. Regular, frequent engagement by parents within the school is likely to lead to a greater understanding of the needs of that school, and experience shows that this may become a tipping point beyond which whole school more able provision becomes substantially easier to deliver. Does the school ensure that the curriculum teaches that every culture interprets its history and learning through certain grand narratives and that these, in turn, contribute to the identities of individuals? Does it teach that most people have a range of affiliations, loyalties and sense of belonging? The idea of using the community as curriculum can be a powerful counter to closed or insular environments. National and international competitions can reveal talents that are exceptional not only in a small community, and can therefore open that community's eyes to the talent within. It is important that schools take the responsibility for developing their learners' long-term aspirations beyond as well as within the community.

Using specific activities to demonstrate the impact of, and potential for, parental and community engagement in the school for more able education can also be a powerful motivator. Consider how the school can develop confidence in the community to involve themselves and enhance more able provision while recognising that in many communities some families are more isolated than others. Engage parents, teachers and learners in a three-way dialogue around aspirations, the role of the school, responsibilities for educating, access to opportunities, challenge and support. Discuss how the school can translate current community involvement into greater engagement. Consider the ideas of community as curriculum and school as community and the extent to which these might overlap. Explore how further engagement between the school and the community can be of benefit for more able provision. Treat community as a resource to be nurtured, fed and involved. If the most able children are the flower, their community and family are the roots; one doesn't grow without the other.

What else counts as meaningful difference?

There are several other significant indicators worth thinking about:

Demographics

Where do individual students live? How do they travel to school? Are they living in an isolated area? Which schools have they attended in the past? Is there a link between the answers to these questions and levels of attainment and achievement?

Participation

How often does a particular learner take part in trips and/or enrichment activities provided by the school? Does the learner seem to have an issue with necessary school equipment (bags, pens, sports kit)? Are there noticeable issues with homework completion, such as, access to resources, domestic chores, tiredness?

Correlations

Do the number and frequency of absences reveal any sort of pattern? Is the student one of an identifiable group within the school, perhaps a child of migrant, refugee or seasonal workers? Do we understand, or know who or how to ask about, the needs and values of those groups?

Behaviours

How do learners show or fail to show resilience in the classroom? Do they suppress aspirations or demonstrate a distinct lack of academic aspiration? Are they abrasive with authority and/or resistant to the school's culture? Is there a mismatch between parent/carer and school attitudes? Do they see themselves as outsiders in the classroom – and the school? Do you perceive a problem with self-esteem?

Self-review

As with all aspects of the inclusion agenda, teachers need to be sensitive to issues which (rural) learners may have in developing learning dispositions, such as risk taking, potential gaps in cultural, social and linguistic capital or other factors which may affect their ability to engage fully in challenging learning and in formal assessments. Deciding who is more able in a classroom or school, based on test results, attitude, or obvious ability, will no doubt be good for those individual learners. Teachers and schools generally do pretty well by such students. The trickier problem is who might have been missed. Thinking about individual learners and the factors that may lead us to misperceive their potential might encourage us to address both the effectiveness of our provision and the ways we intervene to release undiscovered ability. Put more plainly, if we define, as some have, the more able student simply as one who is extremely good at learning, how can we make more students good at learning (Eyre, 2007)?

The Institutional Quality Standards (IQS)[3] was a framework designed to do just that: to support schools (and departments) with self-reviewing processes to inform, plan and develop provision for the more able. Underlying throughout is the notion that all children and young people have the right to receive support and challenge, tailored to their needs, interests and abilities. What this meant in practice was: catch-up where necessary; extension where appropriate; an increase in one-to-one tuition; tailoring teaching and providing a curriculum that challenged every student. Emerging out of a personalised climate, the IQS template prompts teachers to ask themselves a series of fairly basic questions, under five broad headings, about their provision for more able learners: teaching and learning strategies, assessment, curriculum entitlement, school or department organisation, and partnerships beyond the school.

With regard to effective teaching and learning strategies the questions are: whether data reveals pockets of underachievement, how much challenge is built into the curriculum, and how aware teachers are of their students' diverse backgrounds. The assessment focus zooms in on the use of data to inform planning and the notice that has been taken of information from a student's previous school. The curriculum should be examined to pay attention to how it caters for more able students and evidence that those students are responding to what has been provided for them. The fourth area on leadership and organisation must explore tracking able students and monitoring their post school destinations: is provision audited and its impact measured; does the school and department have a written policy to guide more able provision; is there an ethos of ambition and achievement; how are staff trained and developed, and what resources are made available to support the more able project? The final lens focuses on school concerns about engaging with families and community, and with learning beyond the classroom.

Thinking through these issues becomes a useful and pervasive framework for thinking, researching and writing about the more able. The guidance for primary schools (DfES, 2006) and a similar document for secondary schools (DfES, 2007) both used the IQS template as a way of presenting the 'general principles' for the effective planning and delivery of provision for the more able. This approach was used later to analyse the experiences of specific sub-groups, for example, children and young people in care (DfES, 2007b) and, even later, to investigate the experiences of teachers and learners in isolated and rural schools (NRN, 2010).

Looking at rurality, achievement and progression for example, the following issues would arise out of the IQS. Analyse whether:

- the attainment of your able rural learners stands comparison with the rest of your school population or with those in similar schools.
- your identified group of rural learners progress in relation to their prior attainment and potential.
- rural learners fit into pockets of underachievement within your school.
- there are rural learners who are high achievers in national tests whose potential has not been recognised or seen in your more able cohort, either as identified within the cohort, or in individual subjects.
- the destinations of your rural learners with regard to schools, employment, higher education reflect the broadest view of potential within your school.

There is a clear need to encourage teachers and schools to see the *big picture*, in relation to the under representation of key submerged groups and how best to identify and address it. In a book about medical practice Atul Gawande encourages his colleagues to *'count something'* (2007). Perhaps this is where we might use those IQS grids to help us to know where we are and where we ought to be going. Gawande argues that we should beware of *'causal intuitions'* about what's going on in our own and our colleagues' classrooms. Generalisations (and mantras) about our intentions and how we are turning them into reality for learners are not enough on their own and we can be misled by the answers. However hard we reflect and think, says Gawande, we must support our conclusions by 'counting something' – being objective, analysing data, observing lessons, using precise feedback *from* students as well *to* them and as a result perhaps, learning things about the impact of teaching and the responses of students that might even turn out to be *counterintuitive* – and who knows where that might lead?

Nevertheless, there is a need to support self-analysis for individual teachers and for department leaders by providing then with hard-edged ways to shape teacher and subject progression. Data and evidence, precise self-evaluation – 'counting something' – might well open the mind to unexpected insights into individual as well as departmental potential.

Notes

1. REAL Project, London G&T available at www.londongt.org/Real; BME National Strategies Guidance available at www.londongt.org.
2. Sources in this section are discussed in more detail in Warwick and Dickenson: *The National Strategies gifted & talented black pupils achievement*; DfES 2008.
3. *The Institutional Quality Standards for Gifted and Talented Education* (2007). We are using the 2010/11 slightly revised version in our discussions here.

References

Ball, S.: *The Education Debate* (2nd ed.); Bristol, UK: The Policy Press 2013.

BME National Strategies Guidance. Available at www.londongt.org.

DfES: *Effective Provision for Gifted and Talented Children in Primary Education*; Ref: 04072-2006.

DfES: *Effective Provision for Gifted and Talented Students in Secondary Education*; Ref: 0083-2007.

DfES: *Guidance on Preventing Underachievement: A Focus on Children and Young People in Care*; Ref: 00873-2007BKT-EN.

Eyre, Deborah: *What Really Works for G&T*; The National Academy for Gifted and Talented Youth 2007.

Fordham and Ogbu: 'Coping with The Burden Of "Acting White"' *Urban Review*, *18*, 1986, pp. 176–206.

Gawande, Atul: *Better: A Surgeon's Notes on Performance*; New York: Picador 2007.

Gillborn, D.: *Racism and Education: Coincidence or Conspiracy?*; Oxford: Routledge 2008.

National Rural Network for Gifted and Talented Education: *Guidance for Rural and Isolated Schools*; London G&T 2010. Available from: www.londongt.org/Rural.

Ogbu, J.: *Minority Education and Caste: The American Educational System in Cross-Cultural Perspective*; Cambridge, MA: Academic Press 1978.

Queensgate, Lord Puttnam of: *Amazing Children Conference*; June 2000.

REAL Project: London G&T. Available at www.londongt.org/Real.

Steele, C. and Aronson, J.: 'Stereotype threat and the intellectual test performance of African Americans' *Journal of Social Psychology, 65, 9*, 1995. pp. 797-811.

The Institutional Quality Standards for Gifted and Talented Education, 2007.

Warwick, I. and Dickenson, M.: *The National Strategies: Gifted & Talented Black Pupils Achievement*; Dfes 2008.

Chapter 6

The long shadow of poverty

Restricted visibility?

The 'Anna Karenina principle' describes any endeavour in which a deficiency in just a single factor dooms it to failure. Derived from Tolstoy's book which begins, '*Happy families are all alike; every unhappy family is unhappy in its own way*', the principle implies that what is good is more elusive than what is bad. What is good reflects a perfect storm of contributors, and the absence of only one of these contributors precludes what is positive, desirable, or worthy. A successful endeavour is one where every possible deficiency has been avoided. If you are unfortunate enough to have lived in a community damaged by poverty and worklessness for several generations then in fact your 'cultural unhappiness' may start to look depressingly similar, and the likelihood of it impacting on any future aspirations extremely high.

An example was provided by Jared Diamond where he discussed why so few animal species have been domesticated (1997). Unless an animal is easy to feed, unless it grows rapidly, unless it breeds readily in captivity, unless it has a benign temperament, unless it does not run away when frightened, and unless it has a stable social hierarchy, domestication is not going to happen. Think horses versus zebras. If we apply this principle to the well-being of people, the conclusion is discouraging. Threats to happiness and life satisfaction are rife, and it takes only one of these problems to be present to bring us down. In contrast, doing well can only occur in special circumstances.

Centuries ago, Aristotle proposed a similar idea in The *Nicomachean Ethics*: '*For men are good in but one way, but bad in many.*' And much more recently, the psychologist Roy Baumeister and his colleagues concluded that 'bad is stronger than good', meaning that bad emotions, bad parents, and bad feedback have more impact than their good counterparts (2001).

Challenging disadvantage is driven by some as a way to close educational gaps, with the aim of advancing economic progress, but it must be about more than material well-being, it addresses basic human justice. We should ask of ourselves as teachers whether what we do in our classrooms and school has us working as social integrators or whether in fact we are social dividers, as we have undoubtedly been in the past, existing to defend the status quo and 'feed the machine' of commerce and industry. Whatever priorities our own national education systems seem to promote, challenging disadvantage changes intellectual landscapes, particularly those of children born into potentially alienated groups. As a recent report makes clear, '*ensuring that the brightest pupils fulfil their potential goes straight to the heart of social mobility, of basic fairness and economic efficiency*' (Ofsted, 2013).

'Innate' underachievement?

In his book *Outliers*, Gladwell makes the point that as a rule, humans tend to cling to the idea that '*success is a simple function of individual merit and that the world in which we all grow up and the rules we choose to write as a society don't matter at all*' (2008). Any meritocracy is a chimera. Essentially success is a complex phenomenon, and many of the generalisations that are made may blind educators to some of the reasons behind what is happening in schools.

Where more able education is not specifically addressed, research evidence indicates that educational progress is '*not so much a question of intellectual merit but rather a question of affluence*', with the most affluent receiving the best education and therefore achieving most highly. This suggests that '*significant intellectual ability continually goes untapped and unnoticed*' (Campbell, Eyre, Muijs, Neelands, & Robinson, 2004). But the simple creation of better opportunities does not in itself ensure that more able students from disadvantaged groups will necessarily rise through the system. Even in an effective school system, where barriers limiting the achievements of able students are removed, poverty of aspiration, combined with limited access to opportunities, will mean that '*those reaping the most benefit will be largely from affluent groups*' (Campbell *et al.*, 2004).

What teachers need to look at is how they can help students from the poorest backgrounds to see themselves in a very different light as learners. If all the time they believe that somehow their failures are innate and unchanging, a core set of attributes that define their very essence, they are pretty much guaranteed to give up. Seligman argues that such students tend to react to negative events by explaining them in terms of the Three Ps: permanent, personal and pervasive (1991). Instead, teachers need to focus on what learners believe is in their locus of control and how their self-perception can be changed, often despite the impact of their background.

A real danger is that the idea that 'poor kids underachieve' has become such a familiar trope that it is now accepted as a given, and that we sympathise with the under-achiever instead of challenging them with why they are under-achieving. Teachers and schools need to recognise that the content of lessons, the means of delivery and all the paraphernalia of monitoring and reporting are actually secondary to the need to give support and encouragement to the most able, to focus in on mindset; in particular to those whose background gives them so little cause for confidence. Without that crucial enabler, all else is wasted effort.

Deficit models of deprivation

The bigger picture about why more disadvantaged children continue to fail is central to education. Since the late nineteenth century there has been an overt global drive to democratise education. This has been fuelled in more recent times by an understanding that although ability is evenly spread across a country's population, achievement is not. There is a new generation of researchers who are looking far more intensively at the components of character as a means of promoting achievement. Tackling this poverty-driven deficit is not only about reaching towards academic excellence, it is about tackling deprivation and working for social justice in every country. The way education can change lives is perfectly illustrated by the fact that when mothers in developing countries are taught to read, child mortality goes down: when they read they are more likely to access health care and, most of all from the point of view of this and following books, when mothers read, their children do better at school (Engels, 2015).

The importance of education as a tool in reducing deprivation has been shown repeatedly in research and through experience, but what needs a greater effort of imagination and understanding is education's crucial role in achieving equality and social justice in countries where things such as health care and social welfare might seem to be *less* of a pressing issue. In many apparently affluent societies there are still children who, because of living a disadvantaged life in an often-disadvantaged community, remain hard to reach in terms of their educational needs. That nineteenth century democratisation of education which began with a pragmatic need to teach children to read and write (and get them out of the factories) is now much more about raising the visibility of those social factors that interfere with our recognition of potential, to dig beneath the limitations of inheritance and community to examine the causes – and in the case of the more able, accept that learners of high ability are present in all neglected, forgotten or overlooked disadvantaged groups.

In more recent times 'narrowing the gaps' between rich and poor, and between the well-educated and the overlooked, has become a political mantra in both the UK and many parts of the world. Considerable energy has gone, and still goes, into translating the idealism expressed by prominent figures such as Malala Yousafzai and others into the day to day pragmatism of politicians and teachers. If we see ourselves as part of this drive towards expanded intellectual landscapes for all students, then addressing the needs of the more able is just as important. Ensuring that despite economic poverty they become *the best they can be* is just as much a matter of social justice as is teaching mothers to read so that they can access health care.

Hidden potential

Before we can narrow gaps between the more and less advantaged more able learners, we must know what the gaps are. Who is most vulnerable and how do we know? Schools are rightly wary of generalising and stereotyping: a positive response to an identified gap in achievement might reveal that an individual learner is similar or very different to their contemporaries – hence the need to look for 'meaningful differences', rather than catch-all sub-group labels which relate to some sort of disadvantage in background, circumstance or the nature of the individual's ability. Our quest to see beneath the disadvantage is made that much more complex when we consider that a marked ability can hide a disadvantage or disability just as much as a disability or disadvantage can mask a student's capacity to achieve. Of course, any widening of our view of the children sitting in our classrooms inevitably leads us to ask questions about the exact nature of their vulnerability. Have we not seen clearly enough those vulnerabilities? Have we not given those students the opportunity to show and develop their abilities? Did we take any notice of the information we received about them from earlier schools? Are we letting a particular and obvious problem mask potential – and does that child achieve something remarkable outside and away from what we ask them to do in school?

It should be more than obvious by now that we should work from the belief that in any school there are likely to be submerged populations of disadvantaged learners whose potential is in danger of being lost or unrecognised. We need to learn, as teachers, how to see beyond the superficial. We need to ask, once we understand just who these students are sitting in front of us, what it is that might be meaningfully different about their learning needs.

Something really important needs saying at this point: material deprivation is not always obvious. It might not be the limited horizons of his or her family that hinders a student's development, or the absence of family, or particular learning issues, or even the untidiness and edginess of their intelligence. It could be (and often is) the struggle that student's family has in surviving on a day to day basis. Poverty, in other words, is often not all that easy to see. In the UK, we can begin to understand the catchment area of a school, and how degrees of poverty might act as a limiting factor to those students' progress, through the data provided by the Income Deprivation Affecting Children Index (IDACI) or we can get some sense of levels of socio-economic deprivation in our school by looking at the numbers of Government provided free school meals (FSM) or at parental history of further education. We need to better understand what those limiting factors actually look like and how they damage.

Why is it always the same students sliding down the same slope to failure?

Unsurprisingly, research suggests that extreme stress compromises our ability to regulate thought. Students facing extreme circumstances require very different kinds of interventions. We know from the analysis of performance tables that poor students are twice as likely to have special educational needs statements, three times as likely to be excluded, and so on. But the less acknowledged common characteristics are the greater likelihood of family and home turbulence, the smaller chance that they will make informed decisions on subject choices and the lack of cultural and social capital to support them. In addition, environmental risks, such as family turmoil and chaos have a huge effect on children's cortisol levels (Tough, 2013). With the absence of buffers, our students are facing waves of emotion that will almost certainly capsize them.

Paul Tough (2012) summarises this well, when he highlights that children who grow up in more stressful environments,

- generally find it harder to concentrate, harder to sit still, harder to rebound from
- disappointment, and harder to follow directions. This has to do with a particular set
- of cognitive skills located in the prefrontal cortex, known as **executive functions**.
- They have been compared to a team of traffic controllers overseeing the functions of
- the brain. Poverty itself does not compromise the executive functioning abilities
- of poor kids. It was the stress that goes along with it.

This is an astute and hugely significant insight.

Resilience and success

In order to propose better programmes for the most able, and to break the link between achievement and poverty, it is necessary to delve deeper. According to Tough, '*two decades of national attention have done little or nothing to close the achievement gap between poor students and their better-off peers'* (2016). Largely thanks to Claxton's (2002) and Dweck's (2007) work, the word 'resilience' has entered into the school vocabulary with real impact. Duckworth, for her part, defines grit as:

> perseverance and passion for long-term goals. Grit entails working strenuously toward challenges, maintaining effort and interest over years despite failure, adversity, and plateaus in progress.
>
> (2016)

Whether we call it self-efficacy, resilience, grit or conscientiousness, does it have an impact on poverty, and if so, can it be taught? In the UK, a report in 2011 for the Department for Education evaluating the UK Resilience Programme, based on the Penn Resiliency scheme, suggested not. Others such as David Didau have argued in stronger terms (2017). He believes that:

> for the majority of school-based character education interventions, we don't really know what the impact has been. It could be that schools have wasted teaching time and added to teachers' workloads to no discernible effect.

Paul Tough's examination of the traits that help get children through school and university are interesting. The three key qualities that tend to lead more disadvantaged students towards sustained success are persistence, follow-through and deferred gratification. These determine who succeeds and who fails, and why. He looks at the new school of research that is focusing on virtues and character traits and asks: how are schools meant to teach these?

Some non-selective schools in the poorer areas of Washington DC and New York take what can appear as a very old-fashioned route to changing their pupils' perception of themselves, awarding small prizes for the tiniest of achievements, presenting these in public and offering perks for any improved effort or sign of growing aspiration, from trips out of school to vouchers cashable in the school's café. As one Principal pointed out, for some of these children it was the first time they had received any reward for getting something right. The nature of the perks was irrelevant. What the children were being taught was that the more you put in the more you got out.

Recently, Tough has written that:

> for all our talk about noncognitive skills, nobody has yet found a reliable way to teach kids to be grittier or more resilient. . . . What is emerging is a new idea: that qualities like grit and resilience are not formed through the traditional mechanics of 'teaching'; instead, a growing number of researchers now believe, they are shaped by several specific environmental forces, both in the classroom and in the home, sometimes in subtle and intricate ways.
>
> (2016)

He now believes that:

> if we want to help children demonstrate these qualities in school, there are two places where we need to change our approach. One is the classroom. The second

is where children's neurobiological identity begins to be formed, long before they ever set foot in kindergarten: the home.

(2016)

In the classroom, he argues that character is built '*not through lectures or direct instruction from teachers but through the experience of persevering as students confront challenging academic work*' (2016). He believes that many children raised in adversity are enrolled in schools where they are frequently disciplined but seldom challenged. At home, the powerful environmental forces that are acting on many low-income children begins in infancy.

How does poverty influence language development?

If disadvantage casts a long shadow[1] over a child's life, then so too does the way we learn to acquire and use language. Michael Rosen would say that the way we do this helps to shape autonomy and agency. In an earlier chapter we talked about how learning helps us to *become ourselves.* When we apply that idea to those learners who face poverty we can see that the language we use and encourage learners to use helps them not simply to become themselves, but *overcome* whatever varieties of self or circumstance they find difficult. By becoming ourselves, we overcome those selves that could limit who we might be.

We keep coming back to the importance of language development, so how does poverty influence language development? Home and school contexts represent different cultures, subcultures, or both, and influence language acquisition in noticeable ways. By the age of three in the USA, children raised by professional parents have heard 13 million words spoken and those with parents on welfare have heard just 10 million (Hart & Risley, 2003). Andrew Sabisky argues that a sceptical eye needs to be cast over any correlational studies that make sweeping claims of causal relationships between parental and child vocabulary size which do not have '*any built-in genetic controls*'. He points out that '*there are always unobserved genetic confounds at play that neither goodwill nor multiple regression can wish away*' (qtd. in Didau, 2015). His point is that the vocabulary sub-test in popular intelligence test batteries is one of the most highly correlated with the G factor. Consequently, if parental vocabulary size is closely correlated with child vocabulary size '*we should not assume that this is due to the detrimental effect of the environment that the parents provide, unless we have somehow controlled for the genotypes that the parents and their offspring share*' (qtd. in Didau, 2015).

Is there a way out of disadvantage through the keyhole of language? Shirley Brice-Heath recognises that different cultures influence language acquisition in different ways (1983). Her research looks at the way families use language and how that usage might predict future school success. Here we take her research, and that of others, as a pertinent clue in our quest to help students to learn better and achieve more. Brice-Heath concludes:

By the time children are three, the ways in which their parents have talked to them has already shaped their intellectual futures.

(1983)

Susan Engel repeats this idea when she writes that, a child's *language environment is a strong predictor of school success* (2013), and Catherine Snow observes that middle class parents are often *semantically contingent* in the way they answer their children's questions and this seems to prepare those children to learn effectively (1983). In other words, in their answers and in their conversation, those parents pay close attention to whatever the child is focused on, and they demand a high level of language use; they do not oversimplify or use childish synonyms but always using the right word for the context. In simple terms, they **add** more elaborate language to what the child has said. It's about, in Engel's words, providing a *linguistic fingerprint* within the family – a *parental culture* of talking, thinking and reading (2013). Replace *parental* with *classroom* and the same things applies.

This idea of semantic contingency is crucial here. Language is important for the *language-based analytic and symbolic competencies upon which advanced education and a global economy depend* (Hart & Risley, 2012). The writers of this observation, Hart and Risley, add that it is no surprise that language deficits can be handed down through generations of a family. Schools and teachers should fight tooth and nail *not* to contribute to that deficit. We talk more about how this idea works in practice in the discussion about parents, but for now we think that all this gives us a powerful lead towards how we teach: cultivate a climate where the exchanges between students and teacher, at whatever level – early years to university – is semantically contingent; provide a high level of language use – subject specific language, resisting synonyms and over simplification, and weaving in more elaborate language as part of the exchange with a student. The whole process of dialogue between teacher and student should not only be about checking for understanding and delivering knowledge, it should aim to lay the foundations for negotiating unfamiliar materials, fluency, confidence and participation and, importantly for this present discussion, chipping away at those barriers caused by poverty.

What else are we meant to do for our most able disadvantaged students?

Some schools have found a three- or five-year repeating pattern in their under-achievers. The pupil in an early year in the school would be not achieving their potential, but individual subject and class teachers would not realise that the child was failing to achieve elsewhere in school, and be unwilling to report on it because as a high-quality professional they would first try and solve the problem on their own. When individual intervention failed they would blame themselves in part, and not wish to be seen by the Senior Leadership Team as having failed a child in their care. Typically, it could take half a school year for the problem to be recognised and passed on. Measures would then be put in place, but come September and the next school year the record would be wiped clean, new staff would be teaching the child and the entire process of intervention would start again from scratch. Moving in to a new school year may be a rite of passage for the child, but it should be one for which they carry a ticket marked with a record of previous journeys. It is vital to not fall prey to monitoring fatigue. The world is full of schemes for the most able that start with the best of intentions but become tired after one or two years, that tiredness being seen most often in the failure to continue to monitor the progress of set targets, and to hit the alarm button when the targets are not met. Resilience and tenacity of purpose are not only a crucial feature for the success of the child, but for the success of teachers and the school, too.

It is also important to analyse the ambition of the targets set for these students, the progress being made in subjects in comparison to others, the behaviour records, the subject sets, the participation and mobility rates, the parental support and involvement (such as attendance at parents' meetings or student learning review days) as well as the previous destination data or work experience/internships.

Triangulated interviews involving the students themselves, their parents and teachers, can open some fascinating areas. Such interviews will often also bring up the key wider barriers to attainment. Issues to do with behaviour and home background, overcrowding, drug abuse, domestic violence or worklessness. What are the perceived barriers to achievement, the broader concerns, their views on what would help them most? What were parental experiences of school like? Inevitably this widens out the debate and often leads directly into the areas where 'soft' skills (that group together under the rubric of self-regulation) such as optimism, resilience and social agility can be encouraged, as can ambition, confidence and aspiration. These can be the real game changers that help students to deal with the inevitable stresses and rebuffs of their own lives. Off the shelf is worse than useless. Doing what you have always done is probably not that smart either. So, ask. Pupils. Teachers. Parents.

Concerted cultivation

Having touched on the impact of poverty on language development, what other impacts can appear to be inherent in adverse circumstances? Annette Lareau, in her 2003 study, 'Unequal Childhoods' found when she zeroed in on a selected group of widely differing parents for intensive scrutiny on how they raised their children, she found that there were essentially just two parenting 'philosophies', and they divided almost perfectly along economic class lines. '*The wealthier parents raised their kids one way, and the poorer parents raised their kids another way.*' She referred to the middle-class parents' approach as 'concerted cultivation', which involved a great deal of 'intense scheduling' shuttling children from one activity to the next. Poorer parents tended to follow, by contrast, a strategy of 'accomplishment by natural growth'. She realised that, '*intense scheduling was almost entirely absent from the lives of the poor children*', so the activities these children got involved with was considered by their parents as '*something separate from the adult world and not particularly consequential*' (2013).

So, what are the benefits? To her mind, the poorer children were, '*often better behaved, less whiny, more creative in making use of their time, and had a well-developed sense of independence*'. But in terms of their school work, the difference was marked. Although the wealthier students had little or no threshold for suffering or real resilience, they acted as though they had, '*a right to pursue their own individual preferences and to actively manage interaction*' in institutional settings. By contrast, the working-class and poor children were characterised by '*an emerging sense of distance, distrust and constraint*' (2013). Apart from the obvious additional exposure to experiences and cultural capital that go along with this kind of parenting, middle-class parents also were seen to intervene far more on behalf of their children if grades started to slide, unlike the more passive poorer parents who seem to view the authority on display in schools as intimidating. The more middle-class parents also discussed issues with their children and offered them strategies to cope with stress, and to negotiate challenging circumstances. What is really being offered here is

a kind of social agility, as well as the ability to resist and perhaps even oppose passivity and any attempts to make one a victim.

Success and stress

Perhaps the issue of unequal childhoods is even more fundamental. Paul Tough (2016) argues that:

> [a] crucial role that parents play early on is as external regulators of their children's stress. When parents behave harshly or unpredictably – especially at moments when their children are upset – the children are less likely over time to develop the ability to manage strong emotions and respond effectively to stressful situations. By contrast, when a child's parents respond to her jangled emotions in a sensitive and measured way, she is more likely to learn that she herself has the capacity to cope with her feelings, even intense and unpleasant ones.

School can often be the only counterbalancing factor in many learners' lives. A place of safety where the reactions of adults doesn't set all of their alarm bells ringing and cortisol levels soaring.

Although some of the more extreme degrees of disadvantage might seem to be intractable, the real positive to take from the situation is that unlike IQ, which appears to be resistant to any significant changes after the age of eight, executive functions can seriously be worked on. As Tough comments: '*helping children learn a different kind of skill: controlling their impulses, staying focused on the task at hand, avoiding distractions and mental traps, managing their emotions, organising their thoughts the ability to handle stress and manage strong emotions*' can be improved well into adolescence (2016). The most important element is that we address the issues that our schools actually face. Someone else's solution is just that – and usually about as effective on performance as drawing 'go faster' stripes on the side of a car.

What is quite clear is that for many learners who have grown up in highly adverse conditions, the choices that they make can seem to be in total opposition to what we as teachers might perceive as their own self-interest. It looks and feels like self-sabotage. Whatever we can do to help our students to regulate their immediate responses to some situations (which can often appear aggressive and confrontational) must help them to attain their real potential. In 2012, Camille Farrington published a report which talked about the centrality of academic perseverance – the tendency to maintain positive academic behaviours despite setbacks. What that report found was that there wasn't a way of teaching some essential character trait called grit, to help your students to be gritty in the sense of developing a generic character trait. But as a teacher it was possible to help your students to behave in gritty ways in your classroom, in your subject. To allow them to see themselves and possibly the world around them in different ways, which allowed greater autonomy and helped to unleash new positive behaviours.

Note

1. This is a term used by J. Kagan and N. Sidman in *The Long Shadow of Temperament*; Belknap Books New York 2009.

References

Aristotle: *Nichomachean Ethics*; London: Penguin Classics 2004.

Baumeister, R.F., Bratslavsky, E., Finkenauer, C., & Vohs, K.D.: 'Bad is stronger than good'; *Review of General Psychology*, 5, 2001. pp. 323–370.

Brice-Heath, Shirley: *Ways with Words*, Cambridge: Cambridge University Press 1983.

Campbell, R.J., Eyre, D., Muijs, R.D., Neelands, J.G.A., & Robinson, W.: *The English Model: Context, Policy and Challenge*; NAGTY Occasional Paper 1, 2004.

Department of Education: *UK Resilience Programme Evaluation: Final Report* (DFE-RR097); 2011.

Diamond, J.: *Guns, Germs, and Steel: The Fates of Human Societies*; New York: Norton 1997.

Didau, D.: 'Is resilience even a thing?' 2017. Available at: www.learningspy.co.uk/featured/resilience-even-thing/#more-11027.

Didau, D.: *What If Everything You Know About Education Is Wrong?*; Carmarthen, UK: Crown House Publishing, June 2015.

Engel, Susan: *The Hungry Mind: The Origins of Curiosity in Childhood*; Cambridge, MA: Harvard 2013.

Farrington, C.: 'Teaching Adolescents to Become Learners' *University of Chicago Consortium on School Research*, 2012.

Gladwell, M.: *Outliers: The Story of Success*; New York: Hatchette Book Group 2008.

Hart, B. and Risley, T.: *Meaningful Differences in the Everyday Experiences of Young American Children*; Cambridge: Pearson 2012

Kagan, J. and Sidman, N.: *The Long Shadow of Temperament*; Cambridge, MA: Belknap Books 2009.

Lareau, Annette: *Unequal Childhoods: Class, Race and Family Life*; Oakland, CA: University of California 2003.

Ofsted: *The Most Able Students: Are They Doing as Well as they Should in our Non-Selective Secondary Schools?*; Ofsted 2013.

Rosen, M.: blog. http://micahelrosenblog.blogspot.co.uk.

Seligman, M. *Learned Optimism*; New York: A.A. Knopt 1991.

Snow, Catherine: 'Literacy and Language: relationships during the pre-school years'; *The Harvard Educational Review*, 1983.

Tolstoy, L.: *Anna Karenina*; Ware, UK: Wordsworth Classics 1995.

Tough, P.: *How Children Succeed; Grit, Curiosity and the Hidden Power of Character*; London: Random House 2012.

Tough, P.: 'How Kids Really Succeed'; *The Atlantic* 2016. Available at: www.theatlantic.com/magazine/archive/2016/06/how-kids-really-succeed/480744/.

Chapter 7

What research tells parents
Accompanied or alone?

So, complacency & lethargy??

More able students sometimes have trouble connecting personal effort to achievement, seeing it as something beyond their control. Perhaps the reason for this is that much of what they do and learn can be achieved with relatively little effort. While this may seem to be a good position to occupy it has its drawbacks. If they succeed, they might attribute that success to luck or some other external factor outside their control. As a result, they can feel that effort is pointless. Praising of effort from parents and teachers can help, but this needs to be coupled with some attempt by adults to help those students understand the role personal responsibility plays in the whole business of success. A much-admired writer and researcher on the subject is Carol Dweck – and there would be no harm in beginning this chapter with what she says about praise (2006):

Locus of control

> If parents want to give their children a gift, the best thing they can do is to teach their children to love challenges, be intrigued by mistakes, enjoy effort, and keep on learning. That way, their children don't have to be slaves of praise. They will have a lifelong way to build and repair their own confidence.

Her words have impact on us because that great phrase, '*slaves of praise*' no doubt resonates with us, whether we are parents or teachers. Guy Claxton underlines Dweck's point when he says that although talent is important, so is getting things wrong. The important thing is maintaining task commitment and persistence:

> An issue that has to be faced is that learning capacity is as much a matter of character as it is of skill. Being able to stay calm, focused and engaged when you don't know what to do is not a matter of technical training. It requires a self-concept that has not been infected by the pernicious idea that being confused and making mistakes means you are stupid.
>
> (2002)

*Persistence
Curiosity
Self-control*

We talked a good deal about 'character' in Chapter 5 where we referred to what Paul Tough says are most important *set of qualities* to nurture (2013):

*Conscientiousness
Grit
Self-confidence*

> What matters most in a child's development, research says, is not how much information we can stuff into their brain in the first few years. What matters, instead, is whether we are able to help them develop a very different set of qualities, a list that includes persistence, self-control, curiosity, conscientiousness, grit and self-confidence.

Parents will understand this. They might not have a clue about quadratic equations or the periodic table, but they do know about how character works and they will know that, consciously or otherwise, much of what they try to achieve with their children is a list of qualities that very much echo Tough's *set of qualities*.

In the Glossary, we have assembled a whole collection of what we believe are usable ideas from recent research, all of which should begin to answer questions about how we support the development of our children as effective learners. Some of those ideas are worth a brief mention here before we go on to stress what we think is the biggest contribution parents make to their child's learning: how they encourage the use and development of language.

The American psychologist, Robert Bjork coined the phrase, *desirable difficulties* to describe the importance of encouraging students to find ways to deal with challenging work (2011). As a result, they learn to process their learning at a deeper level and, in the end, find retention easier. Elsewhere we talk a lot about *cultural capital* and *priming the pump*. Without a steady flow of information, experience and knowledge there is a danger that learners will mend up *running on empty*. Hence the importance of providing learners with experiences and knowledge. Motivation, according to this view, is driven by achievement: knowing and being able to do stuff make us want to know and do more. One last idea, out of that lengthy Glossary list, *mental contrasting*. Parents need to help their children to think through failure by embarking on a dual process of imagining what might go well but also imagining what might go wrong, and how to deal with that.

Relishing challenge, building capacity, acknowledging failure and foregrounding the importance of character qualities are all important, but the idea that we find more persuasive than most is a concept known as **semantic contingency**. The phrase comes from Catherine Snow (1983). She writes about how children from poor families have difficulty learning to use language to describe things, construct arguments and solve abstract problems – in short, to use academic language. Some learners, not just the materially deprived, hear talk in their families that is almost entirely transactional: 'your dinner's ready'; 'put your clothes away'; 'time you went to bed' and so on; business talk, which for the most part simply tells them what to do. In other, perhaps more middle-class families, the talk is what she calls, *semantically contingent* – parents respond to what the child says in ways which focus closely on the language the child has used, and in the process, draws attention to the variety of language and encourages higher levels of response. This sort of talk encourages reflection, conversation, extended responses, a greater variety of conversational formats and, in the end, more practice at finding the most effective ways to communicate how we feel, what we need and what we believe.

If we are going to talk with young people, about what is important and what is less important, about how they might deal with whatever issues they might meet, then Snow's perception is of enormous use: we must use language in ways that encourage long and considered conversations! More of this later.

Why does what parents do, or not do, matter so much?

Children need to see that their parents value education. The way they talk about their own relationship to education clearly sends a powerful message to their children.

As a result, they have an enormous potential to undermine or to support the positive messages that schools might be promoting. It is not uncommon for parents to 'shift the blame' for failures past and present onto school and thereby undermine their children's relationship with school and to learning. Another unhelpful and related approach is the 'empathising too much' strategy. This tends to look like the 'I was lousy at Maths too' type statements which not only can suggest that a lack of ability in a subject is inherited, but also that it is likely to be irreversible and is somehow genetically fixed. Another well-meaning but damaging line that parents often take is, 'pre-empting of disappointment'. This tends to look like the 'you'll never be a footballer/pianist/rocket scientist so get used to lower goals' line that undermines ambition. A child who might want to become an astronaut should be told that maths and science are vitally important skills and that studying these subjects will be rewarding even in pursuit of seemingly unattainable goals and interests. They may of course even turn out to be completely attainable.

As well as under-estimating, we sometimes over-estimate. We think able children can manage on their own, that they've got everything going for them, that if they behave incorrectly we should be harsher because they should know better; if they are not constantly challenged, they will get lazy; they should be excused some of the usual rules of the home or the classroom; given their ability they should be mature – academically, emotionally, physically and socially. The truth is that in many ways supporting and developing highly able young people requires exactly as much tightrope walking as managing any other young person. There is just as much to lose.

In a 2014 article about parental support for learning, the *New York Times* reported that:

> Researchers at the University of Texas at Austin and Duke University this year assessed the effect of more than 60 kinds of parental involvement on academic achievement. Across age, race, gender and socioeconomic status, most help had neither a positive or negative effect, and many kinds of parental support drove down a child's test scores and grades.

Sometimes, parents misperceive the maturity of young people and with the best of all possible motives, muddy the waters. Researchers found that one parental activity that had the biggest negative impact was 'homework help'. Through what they intended to be encouragement and support, parents effectively increased their children's dependency on them. In discussions with teachers in many Western countries it becomes very clear that sometimes parents believe that their highly able children are delicate and fragile orchids who require special tending; that they are in danger of burnout and when their child is not getting consistent A's, they must be struggling. It was summed up well by a teacher who commented that her students and parents (in this case in Minnesota) wanted the world **perfectly paved** for their child. This approach is also called **snow ploughing** – parents clearing away all obstacles along their children's path to perfection. In the case of the students of that teacher in Minnesota, snow ploughing produced students who became unable to face difficulties alone and became too passive, gave up too easily, shut down or switched off when subjects got too tricky, lacked drive, did not want to struggle or work hard and found it difficult to problem solve. The fear of failure and of being wrong reduced the likelihood of her students taking on big challenges, and this, in turn, led to narrower life choices. She believed that parents were really to blame, as they supported their children whenever she wanted to make their assignments more challenging.

Apart from asking parents, as the former high mistress of St Paul's independent school in London does, to *not get too involved*, where should parents stand in relation to their child's education? They will almost certainly recognise that idea of cultural capital that we mentioned earlier. By this we mean, giving learning authentic context. Parents do this when they take their children on a visit to the theatre or a national monument, when they share a domestic activity such as cooking, when they talk about what is happening in the news or when they respond to a child's request for more information about whatever has caught their attention.

In these activities and conversations, the responsibility for learning has shifted from the adult to the learner, experiencing and responding is about collaboration not competition or testing. When parents get it right, knowledge is constructed between the adult and the child as well as received, and new knowledge is nurtured. In short, the best thing parents can do to support their child's learning is to **cultivate through conversation** which should mean: *the ability to hold doubt, suspend judgement, and take in new information for an extended period of time*.

In other words, rather than simplify, accept that there are many unanswered questions. It isn't hard to do and is the most rewarding of approaches for parents, if not teachers, to take:

> Rather than disciplining children to learn, why not create conditions where the child is hungry for knowledge.
>
> (Engel, 2013)

Books, books, books – and the language of learning

Following an extensive series of meetings and discussions with practising teachers, in 2016, London Gifted and Talented produced short paper entitled, *What are the areas emerging from the surveys as 'problematic' regarding A★ teaching and learning in English?* Partly about the Oxbridge entrance tests, partly about need for a structured agenda for reading, partly about the whole notion of 'high challenge' for those students with '*creative, edgy, untidy intelligences*' the paper is in fact mostly about how:

> The key barrier is the lack of appropriately deep and broad reading experience at a sufficient level of challenge. This takes many years to build up (dating back to KS2 and perhaps having its roots in parental reading culture before that) and cannot be instantaneously created when students begin AS courses.

What the process found was that students' reading experience had clearly 'atrophied' over time so that their sensitivity to challenging texts and their ability to respond to them increasingly faded.

Reading with children or talking to young people about books is an important, not to say pleasurable and unstressful way to support them. It is not just an effective way to bond and engage with young people – of course it's that – but there is clearly a problem if a student's 'reading culture' wanes in early adolescence. If this happens, picking up the threads of regular reading when it is much needed leading up to examinations becomes much harder. Books provide an opportunity for talk – questions, dialogue, sharing opinions, justifying those opinions, identifying issues, summarising content, making connections with other books or experiences and articulating responses. Most of all, like eating together, it cements relationships.

How do we scaffold that reading experience from an early age? How do we, parents and teachers, create those:

> habits of thought, reading, writing, and speaking which go beneath surface meaning . . . to understand deep meaning, root causes, social context, ideology, and personal consequences of any action, event, organisation, experience, text, subject matter, policy, mass media or discourse.
>
> (Shor, 1999)

How do we move on from accessing knowledge in a 'mechanical' way with an emphasis on 'decoding' rather than shades of meaning? How can we usher students into a place where they can not only read the words, but can interpret them? Learning language, learning through language and learning about language all involve learning to *understand things in more than one way*. We learn in a 'multimodal' way. Questions, interaction, finding ways to scaffold understanding, talking about vocabulary, comprehension, developing confidence, fluency, participating in stories, inference and most of all, interpretation are not simply about reading aloud, they are about dialogue; it's not simply about checking for understanding and delivering knowledge, it's about testing and questioning experience. It's laying the foundations for negotiating unfamiliar materials, which is exactly what A★ (and Oxbridge interviewers) require all those years later.

Michael Rosen has written a short and super-concise piece on his blog called, *How does 'reading for pleasure' do its magic?*. What he says is useful for parents and more than useful for teachers. It gives us a framework for a discussion about how we *generate* the sort of readers *who can understand things in more than one way*. Rosen's point about the importance of exposing children to lots of books is reminiscent of an influential 1969 book by Daniel Fader called, *Hooked on Books*. Fader's message was simple – saturation: books, magazines, newspapers, articles, and comics – anything containing the written word. Rosen insists that this process of reading 'scatteringly' (to transpose Montaigne's phrase about learning) is about:

> *how language is stuck together in sentences and paragraphs* and *how ideas are structured and carried through in fiction, non-fiction, drama, poetry, graphic novels and the like.*

Like Fader, Rosen stresses that it doesn't matter how much you *teach* things like vocabulary and grammar, unless they are exposed to that whole variety of reading experiences, children are unlikely to 'get it' in a way that influences how they write and think for themselves.

This isn't just about English either: subject teachers and parents, and the array of reading materials (books, journals, articles, DVDs) they offer in their classrooms and on their bookshelves, can make an enormous difference too.

Fader's idea of word-saturation would almost certainly for him include the internet and screen time had it been around when he wrote his book. In their 2015 book *Make*

Every Lesson Count, Allison and Tharby similarly embrace the potential of the internet, not just for quick answers to factual puzzles, but as an invitation into deeper study. They recommend:

1. Introducing students to subject specific websites such as BBC Science or National Geographic.
2. Posting selected QR codes around a room – depending on the current area of interest: these are those small rectangles full of wavy lines that appear on advertisements and increasingly in information books. A smartphone links the user to a website.
3. Teachers might set up subject-specific Twitter or Facebook accounts as a way of providing links to useful web pages.
4. Explore the online tool at: https://padlet.com/ – a safe and reliable way of chasing down connections and ideas.
5. Set up a subject-specific blog (look up WordPress: easy to access and use) where students can contribute articles and information (much more fun than homework in exercise books).

Back to Rosen, and back to Shirley Brice-Heath in her *Ways with Words*: stories invite us to talk about morals and virtue, about right and wrong. This requires us to *interpret*, not only the characters and their actions, but the way the writer describes those characters and their actions, their feelings and their thoughts. Rosen says that reading is *potentially a gateway into developing our powers of interpretation*. To say, as tests often do, that reading is simply about retrieval and inference is like saying 2+2 doesn't add up to anything.

We never know for certain why the writer did this or that, there isn't one perfect 'ideal' reader who is affected by the metaphor or the alliteration in the way that the examiner thinks this ideal reader is affected. This narrows the potential of writing to enable and foster interpretation. To get to that point we should go with the flow of the writing, and explore how we think and feel – and why. Finding the links to other things we've read and our own life experience and back to the writing in question is one way of doing that.

Rosen concludes that readings is *how we develop our autonomy and agency . . . and in doing so, we get more confident to surf, scan, 'plunder' texts for what we need and want* (2016). Our children need to be surrounded by books in their bedroom, playroom, study, house, so that maybe, in later life, their books from childhood and adolescence might represent something like this:

> *Every library is autobiographical . . . our books will bear witness for or against us; our books reflect who we are and what we have been. . . . What makes a library a reflection of its owner is not merely the choice of the titles themselves, but the mesh of associations implied in that choice.*
>
> (Manguel, 2006)

The poet Tony Harrison talks about his childhood relationship with his father being full of silences and sullen looks, but those tensions do not dominate his memory (2016). What matters most in their relationship is, books, books, books. Wouldn't it be great if we could say the same?

Strategies for parents

It must be clear by this point in this chapter, about and for parents, that we see language development as a key factor in how children and young people are both supported and extended:

> *Particular forms and uses of language are intimately tied to certain cogitative processes. The child who practices reminiscing develops an extended self. The child who practices decontextualized language is more capable of decontextualized thinking. Similarly, the child who asks questions that get answered, and hears others asking questions, not only learns to ask questions, but also develops the disposition to wonder about things and to actively seek answers from others.*[1]

If research has told us a good deal about the importance of conversations and how they work, and about how vital language development is to academic success in every area of learning, then it has also told us a good deal about the importance of the emotional strategies that parents should engage with in order to support their children – and the school. They could help their children to see that grappling with challenges is more important than any amount of easy success. They should try not to fixate on grades as a measure of worth. They could also ensure that their children don't see the act of trying itself as a demonstration of their stupidity or failure. They should give as much responsibility as they believe they can regarding behaviour and learning, and thereby offer their children the opportunity to be trusted, while avoiding soft rewards that can undermine high expectations. As we said in the chapter on underachievement, extrinsic (goal-oriented) motivation is okay some of the time, but intrinsic (curiosity or interest driven) motivation pays much higher dividends – which is another way of saying, try not to impose your own judgements of what is relevant or not on your child. Genuine interest gives a child a momentum that comes in useful in lots of circumstances.

In terms of academic strategies, they should try not to accept their child's first responses too quickly but ask them to justify their opinions as thoroughly as they can. In turn, they should try not to over-simplify their own explanations. If, as was suggested earlier in this chapter, a political situation being discussed is complex, parents should go into as much detail as they can to show that there are hugely ambiguous situations in the world that defy easy explanations. They should obviously try not to praise talent before effort and try not to come to the rescue of their child way before they need to. This is how children learn.

Parents, and teachers, need to remind themselves how important it is for the most able young people to be presented with questions, issues and problems to which there is no answer, and certainly no easy one. Parents also need to have reinforced to them the basic truth that a person must experience failure and disappointment if they are to learn to cope with it.

And – before we move on – something the then high mistress of St Paul's said to parents – particularly those parents who hold down demanding jobs:

> *You cannot use the same technology that you deploy at work to parent your children. Email and text messages cannot replace a hug or a cup of tea at the right time. . . . We are deceiving ourselves if we think that we can bring up children through an iPhone. You can't make an*

appointment for children. If they have a problem and they want to talk to you about it, that's when you have to be prepared to set aside your own agenda and listen.

(Farr, 2017)

A post script for parents and teachers: understanding the school's community

Language is one of the all-time windows onto variation between nations, communities and individual families.

(Engel, 2013)

Shirley Brice-Heath's *Ways with Words* (1983) is a research project into how a White working-class community used reading as a way of teaching values and morals, and a Black working-class community in the same town used reading primarily to intensify interpersonal relationships. Miller, Potts and Fung (1990) compared the ways in which Taiwanese and European–American families socialised their children through story telling: in Taiwan, the children were encouraged to listen, while the U.S. families encouraged participation.

It is quite possible that our children share a classroom with White and Black working class, Asian, European, African, Australasian and American children, all with differing 'linguistic fingerprints'. We are not raising this point as a way of saying that parents and teachers should become language analysts or that they should feel challenged by such a rich mix, simply that, alongside having a clear understanding of the importance of language in every school subject, they should be aware that in classrooms and surrounding streets there is an array of 'ways with words' – even in what might appear to be geographically quite a small and even homogeneous community.

Schools want parents to 'hear' what they are saying about their aspirations and methods; parents need schools to hear their 'voice' too. Mutual understanding and a sensitivity to language supports dialogue. We said earlier that we need to see our work in schools as urgent and immediate, dynamic, holistic and practical. This applies not just to the way we do our work in the classroom, but also to our relationships in our homes and with the communities we share – and those relationships are built on dialogue. Parents and teachers won't understand each other unless we find occasions for dialogue, not just parents' evening, but sharing the work of experts, workshops on aspects of learning for the more able, using parental expertise in the school – and even – teachers setting, and parents asking for, homework that invites parental participation!

Note

1.   This is a digest of research by Neisser (1988), Cole, Scribner, and Souberman (1978).

References

Allison, S. & Tharby, A.: *Making Every Lesson Count: Six Principles to Support Great Teaching and Learning*; Carmarthen, UK: Crown House Publishing 2015.

Brice-Heath, S.: *Ways with Words*; Cambridge: Cambridge University Press 1983.

Claxton, Guy: *Building Learning Power: Helping Young People Become Better Learners*; Bristol, UK: TLO Ltd 2002.

Dweck, C.: *Mindset: The New Psychology of Success*; London: Random House 2006.

Engel, S.: *The Hungry Mind*; Cambridge, MA: Harvard 2013.

Fader, D.: *Hooked on Books*; New York: Mass Market Paperback 1976.

Farr, C.: 'Interview with Sian Griffiths'; *The Sunday Times* March 2017.

Harrison, T.: *Bookends, Collected Poems*; London: Penguin 2016.

London Gifted and Talented: 'What are the areas emerging from the surveys as "problematic" regarding A★ teaching and learning in English?'; 2016. Available at: http://londongt.org/#publication.

Manguel, Angel: *The Library at Night*; New Haven, CT: Yale 2006.

Miller, P.J., Potts, R. and Fung, R.H.: 'Narrative practices and the social construction of self in child'; *American Ethnologist* 1990.

Neisser, U.: *Five Kinds of Self-Knowledge*. 1998. Available at: https://edocs.uis.edu/Departments/LIS/Course_Pages/LIS301/papers/Self_Knowledge.pdf

Newman, J.: '"But I Want to Do Your Homework", Helping Kids With Homework'; *The New York Times*, Sunday Review, June 21, 2014.

Rosen, Michael: 'How does 'reading for pleasure' do its magic?' http://michaelrosenblog.blogspot.co.uk/2016/03/how-does-reading-for-pleasure-do-its.html.

Cole, M., John-Steiner, V., Scribner, S. and Souberman, E. (eds): *Mind in Society: The Development of Higher Psychological Processes*; Cambridge, MA: Harvard University Press 1978.

Snow C.E.: 'Literacy and Language: Relationships during the preschool years'; *Harvard Educational Review* 1983.

Tough, P.: *How Children Succeed: Grit, Curiosity and the Hidden Power of Character*; Wilmington, NC: Mariner Books 2013.

Tough, P.: 'Academic Language and the challenge of reading for learning about science'; *Science* 2010.

Part two

Chapter 8

Whose classroom is it anyway?

Seating allocations?

How you organise your children is of fundamental importance.

(IESR, 2001)

What lies behind the decisions a school makes about who sits where in which classroom? Is the way children are grouped driven by a priority to ensure effective learning and progress for all students, or is the underlying purpose much more to do with challenging social hierarchies? When a school chooses to group children of similar ability together (stream), or to place children of similar ability together for certain subjects (set) or to teach the whole span of attainment in one room, irrespective of ability (mixed ability – which expects that teachers will manage the spread of attainment using in-class grouping and differentiation) or even to teach boys and girls separately (as is now happening more and more) what is their motivation for such a decision – and what are the consequences?

This book began with an insistence that what happens in schools ought to be driven by *the fierce urgency of now*. Whose urgency do we mean? Whose needs are we meeting? When we stream, or set, or teach in mixed ability groups, whose interests are we furthering? Are these interests – school, parents, society, the individual student – compatible and/or interchangeable. Is there anyone who can tell schools and teachers, definitively, which approach is the more effective?

Up until the 1960s in the UK, in schools where pupil numbers allowed, setting and streaming were the norm. The turning point came with the Plowden Report's[1] emphasis on the importance of child-centred education and this led, among other things, to an increase in mixed ability teaching, particularly in primary schools. For more than twenty years this then became the norm until, from the mid-1990s onwards, setting and streaming began to make a comeback.

The IESR report quoted at the top of this chapter concludes that mixed ability grouping has the edge because it has a measurable impact on a reduction of under-achievement, while at the same time there are clear *social and equitable benefits*. As far as the teaching of mathematics was concerned: *The expectation of greater gain by schools choosing to set by ability was not supported by figures; in fact, the results supported a tentative conclusion by the authors that children at all levels of attainment do better when taught in mixed ability groups* (IESR, 2001). Their research shows that pupils in mixed ability classes made up to a 7% average gain in test scores over those learners taught in sets, but they do add – and this is perhaps an important 'but' – most of those gains were made by children of lower ability because *they observe how others approach problem-solving and calculating in mathematics.*

IESR concludes that, *policies of setting were adapted primarily to make teacher' tasks more manageable*. This would tally with an observation made by the UK's former Chief Inspector of School, Sir Michael Wilshaw, when he talked about, *the curse of mixed ability classes without mixed ability teaching* (qtd. in Paton, 2012). We will return to this thought later.

Other studies have followed this mathematics-specific one from IESR. In 2012 Beatriz Pont's study for the Organisation for Economic Co-operation and Development[2] found that streaming *exacerbates* inequalities for pupils from low-income and immigrant families, and that countries where pupils were divided at an early age tended to have higher numbers of drop outs and lower levels of attainment. This was followed in 2014 by a report by Susan Hallam and Samantha Parsons, which concluded that *the widespread use of streaming will do little or nothing to arrest the difficulties faced by children from disadvantaged backgrounds and those whose parents have a low level of education* and was, in fact, *likely to be counterproductive in reducing the attainment gap* (2014).

Jeannie Oakes' work in the US tracks students set or streamed into ability groups and finds, like the studies already mentioned, that those organisational structures further limit individual students and, more than that, perpetuate inequalities of race and class (2005). Teachers' expectations for students tend to be shaped by the initial groupings and confining students to rigid tracks leads teachers to devote fewer resources to low-achieving students. Oakes notes that concerns in other studies about ability grouping focus on the inequalities that can inadvertently arise when students are separated by ability, as the process often results in students from disadvantaged backgrounds being under-represented in more able groups. Thus, streaming might well act as a force of societal polarisation. Inequality is perpetuated by trapping poor and minority students in low-level groups, resulting in life patterns for many children laid down at a very early age. These are social arguments that have some legitimacy and force.

For a fair number of educationalists and researchers, Martin Luther King's phrase *the fierce urgency of now* (used in a speech called 'Beyond Vietnam: A Time to Break Silence' April 1967) might well be applied to describe the pressing and immediate need to address society's inequalities through what happens in our schools. The Sutton Trust, in their report on ways that funding might be allocated in order to raise achievement (The Pupil Premium), concluded that ability grouping had very low or negative impact, and as a strategy it comes very near to the bottom of their list of the most effective ways to raise achievement.

When we asked, at the start of this chapter, what lies behind the decisions about who sits where in which classroom, we suggested that it could be about challenging social hierarchies, but it could also be about the precise needs of individual students in terms of realising their potential. We implied that meeting the needs of an individual and addressing the shortcomings of society might not always be quite the same thing. The 'interests' that a grouping policy responds to might be social, but equally, they could be individual. In short, narrowing society's gaps in terms of educational attainment might not prove to be a complete answer to the needs of *all* young people.

As Michael Rosen put it (2016):

> Social mobility . . . is the process by which people in lower groups rise to the higher ones. As "mobility" doesn't include the word "rising" it could, in theory mean "falling". In fact, if people are to rise, don't the same number have to fall?

Railing against streaming and setting and promoting mixed–ability grouping inevital poses questions about who might be harmed, who might 'fall' as well as who might 'ris

Supporters of mixed ability grouping would argue that able students can act as r models for other students, as that piece of research into Mathematics grouping showed; Joseph Renzulli seems to agree with this in his famous phrase, *a rising tide lifts all ships* (1998). For Renzulli, the *rising tide* is the more able learners who are there to lift everyone else – *all ships* a powerful metaphor for inclusiveness. He doesn't seem to have coined a phrase to do with able learners needing to be in the company of other able students, however.

In the minds of earlier generations, success in education was indelibly linked to success in life. Not being in the top sets or streams (and certainly not being in the 'right' school) would seem to imply that you were *doomed to be second-class, not just educationally, but socially and economically* (Davies, 2016). We have come to accept an ineradicable link between what happens in the classroom with what happens in society.

The trouble is, we have struggled to find a way to *lift all ships*, to ensure that *all children reach their potential*. Mixed-ability teaching might have seemed a good bet, but for teachers to do it well is, as Sir Michael Wilshaw says, '*hugely difficult*'. He calls much of what he has seen in the UK's schools, '*the curse of mixed-ability classes without mixed ability teaching*'. He expands this by adding that, '*where there are mixed-ability classes, unless there is differentiated teaching, it doesn't work*' (qtd. in Paton, 2012). In bald terms, he believes that schools have moved away from a motivation to develop and hone *good practice*, towards a conviction that mixed-ability grouping will enhance our key purpose of enabling *social engineering*.

The Hallam and Parsons (2014) report mentioned earlier contains a striking observation:

> Children in the top stream achieved more and made significantly more academic progress than children attending schools that did not stream while children in the bottom streams achieved less and made significantly less academic progress.

So, the more able do better when streamed, the less able do worse when streamed. As a result, differences between abilities, and by implication between backgrounds, are accentuated.

If we believe this analysis – and the Sutton Trust and IESR would challenge this conclusion with some firmness, saying that high and average ability students do not appear to suffer from mixed-ability teaching (simply from a limited capacity to learn independently) – then pushing harder for a mixed-ability solution has a limited chance of working.

Many teachers find such a method of organising learning just too hard.

Able students need each other's company, they relish interactive strategic and analytic activities; they enjoy a high challenge competitive environment. The trick would be, in a mixed-ability environment, to react to those needs without intimidating those students with dissimilar needs. Skilful differentiation allows bright, average, and slower youngsters to profit from in-class grouping programmes that adjust the curriculum to the aptitude levels of the various in-class groups. Without that adjustment, some students are harmed, in one way or another.

Ed Baines uses an analysis of existing research to examine what he believes are some myths that have surrounded teaching and learning (2012). Particularly, he trawls through several studies which focus on how children are grouped.[3] Like the more recent research, mentioned earlier, these projects reveal that in mixed-ability situations there is only a marginal effect on the achievement of most students from the way they are grouped, but unlike those earlier European studies, the studies that Baines quotes found that for higher ability students there were much more pronounced advantages from ability grouping – from setting or streaming. Higher ability students made greater progress and were far more likely, in such an environment, to experience an enriched or accelerated curriculum in line with their needs.[4] These enrichment and acceleration programmes have a clear and measurable impact on student learning. In typical evaluation studies, talented students from accelerated classes outperform non-accelerates of the same age and IQ by almost one full year on achievement tests. Talented students from enriched classes outperform initially equivalent students from conventional classes by four to five months on grade equivalent scales.

In his conclusion Baines conclusively states that, just as in those European studies, 'the more able pupils benefit from ability grouping, while the less able are disadvantaged by this approach' (2012).

Whether motivated by expediency or belief, slowly and yet very noticeably, schools are returning to ability grouping. It isn't seen any more as an evil; most estimates now are that more than 60% of all primary schools are doing it. Teachers who use grouping argue that it has become indispensable, helping them to cope with a bewildering mix of strengths and weaknesses and widely varying levels of ability and achievement and also of course, to help them cope with the work load!

Are the horns of this dilemma really about equity versus excellence? Or are we over-simplifying and missing the point? Are there other more immediate issues to consider? If the way we structure schools and classrooms is not a complete answer then thinking about *how* we teach effectively must surely help: structures do not create good practice, there are other things to get right if we are to meet the needs of our most able students.

There is a sometimes unspoken assumption that able children cannot fail: that they come from comfortable and supportive families, have access to private tutoring, regular visits out to see culturally interesting exhibitions and artefacts, and sometimes even stimulating conversations around the dinner table. No wonder they can't fail.

Except of course they do fail. All too frequently. Even these 'heavily supported' students often go off the rails, or misunderstand the demands being made of them or the degree of difficulty of an exam or a university interview, or assume that because they might be top of their class they will automatically get the top grades they need.

When teachers are asked about more able students they reveal just as much anxiety and uncertainty about their progress as they do about the most disadvantaged. They want to understand how to build a culture of excellence throughout their schools, not just leading up to examinations, and want to know, most of all, how best to 'challenge' students so that they have a realistic view of what excellence, real expertise and scholarship looks like, so that, in Will Durant's paraphrase of Aristotle: *We are what we repeatedly do. Excellence, therefore, is not an act, but a habit* (1926).

Of course, there are libraries full of books about how to teach effectively, so what we have to say here is very much a digest of what seem to be some key approaches. The Sutton Trust, in their 'toolkit' that advises schools on how best to spend their money, puts three strategies at the top of their 'best practice' list: effective feedback; meta-cognition and regulation strategies, peer tutoring and peer assisted learning. After extensive research and evidence gathering, John Hattie tops his list with: reciprocal teaching (group work); feedback and meta-cognition (2009). So, putting the two research projects together, best practice happens when we offer opportunities for:

1. Effective feedback.
2. Productive groupwork.
3. Giving students the vocabulary to talk about their own learning.

Barry Hymer (2014) conflates much of this research in a quotation from Vygotsky (1978):

> Every function in the child's cultural development appears twice: first on the social level and later on the individual level; first between people, and then inside the child. All the higher mental functions originate as actual relations between people.

Hymer talks about how able students need the space to transform received examination/curriculum information into an infinite number of new creations, how this process demands understanding as well as performance, and how it needs to encourage connection making. Embedding excellence in the classroom involves lateral and sometimes contradictory ways of thinking, and quality dialogue between peers and between students and teachers. The core value at the heart of everything we do in the classroom, according to Hymer, is a belief that knowledge can be *created* as well as accessed through some ready-made tool.

When schools are inspected in any country, of course performance data will be taken into account (and whether or not students fulfil early potential) but what the inspectors see happening in the classroom is key. They are not interested, we may be surprised to hear, in whether students are organised into streams, or sets or mixed ability groups[5] but they *do* expect to see:

1. Learners achieving beyond what might be expected in a lesson – and in ways their teacher had not predicted.
2. Learners able self-regulate, remain on task, concentrate, work without direction.
3. Resilient learners.
4. Learners who are ambitious to improve and eager to grasp new learning opportunities.
5. Learners who make exemplary progress and exceed expectations.

All this goes some way towards answering questions about 'how' classrooms should work.

London Gifted & Talented, who played a significant role in the impressive results achieved by The London Challenge to 'raise the bar' for all children in London, not least the more able, outlines some ways a teacher might meet the needs of the more able:

1. The introduction to this book talked about 'learning in the present tense'. Present learning as 'live'; stress enquiry and possibility. Use 'could be' language.

2. Model genuine curiosity yourself; admit when you don't know and discuss how you might find out. Share your passion for learning.
3. Take learners 'behind the curtain' of the learning to explain why we are doing this today and who it's for.
4. 'Easy is boring; impossible is depressing . . . '. Engage with intriguing subject matter. Explore the concept of 'desirable difficulty' explored later in this series.
5. Develop speculative learning projects: go off-piste, embrace tangents and awkward questions.
6. Create intriguing hooks. What if? Think out loud. Post questions. Make trailers.
7. Respond to real world problems.

Later we will talk about the importance of persistence and resilience as crucial 'default' positions in the pursuit of excellence, and about how a student's work needs to be underwritten by a clear expectation regarding accuracy and precision in the use of elevated levels subject specific language. The importance of language as a way of achieving precision of explanation and thought echoes not just through this book but through all the books in this series. The reward is improved motivation through the learning; students wanting to develop their subject knowledge, wanting to learn per se, rather than just to do well in exams. As Michael Marland said, a long time ago now, motivation – and aspiration – happen for the most part because of achievement (2002).

So – is the way you *organise* your children of fundamental importance or is the way you *teach* your children at least, if not more, important?

Notes

1   The Plowden Report: about Primary School organisation and curriculum; published 1967 by the Central Advisory Council for Education.
2   See Jessica Shepherd in *The Guardian* February 2012: 'Dividing younger pupils by ability can entrench disadvantage, study finds.' OECD Study by Beatriz Pont: *Equity and Quality in Education: Supporting Disadvantaged Students.*
3   See Kulik, J.A., and Kulik, C.L.: 'Timing of Feedback and Verbal Learning.' *Review of Educational Research 58* 1988; Slavin, R: *Cooperative Learning*; Allyn & Bacon 1995.
4   Out of hours learning is seen by many schools as an essential part of what they offer; enhancing but not replacing school based learning in ways that *increase motivation, self-esteem and, in the long term the attainment of individuals* (Eyre: *What Really Works*; University of Warwick 2007).
5   In the UK inspectors are told that 'they must not expect teaching staff to teach in any specific way or follow a prescribed methodology'.

References

Baines, E.: *Bad Education: Debunking Myths in Education*; Oxford University Press 2012.
Central Advisory Council for Education: *The Plowden Report*; 1967.
Davies, H.: *The Co-op's Got Bananas*; London: Simon and Schuster 2016.
Durant, W.: *The Story of Philosophy: The Lives and Opinions of the Greater Philosophers*; London: Simon & Schuster 1926.
Eyre, D.: *What Really Works*; Warwick, UK: University of Warwick 2007.
Hallam and Parsons: 'The impact of streaming and attainment at age 7: evidence from the Millennium Cohort Study'; *Oxford Review of Education* 2014.
Hattie, J.: *Visible Learning*; London: Routledge 2009.
Hymer, B.: *Growth Mindset Pocketbook*; Teachers' Pocketbooks 2014.

Institute of Economic and Social Research, The (IESR) 'Effective Organisation in Primary Schools'; *Mathematics* 2001.

Kulik, J.A. and Kulik C.L.: 'Timing of Feedback and Verbal Learning.' *Review of Educational Research*, Vol. 58 (1998).

Marland, M.: *The Craft of the Classroom*; London: Heinemann 2002.

Oakes, J.: *Keeping Track: How schools structure inequality*; New Haven, CT: Yale University Press 2005.

Paton, G.: 'Ofsted: mixed-ability classes 'a curse' on bright pupils'; *Daily Telegraph* September 2012.

Pont, B.: *Equity and Quality in Education: Supporting Disadvantaged Students*; OECD.

Renzulli, J.S.: 'A Rising Tide Lifts All Ships: Developing the Gifts and Talents of All Students'; *The Phi Delta Kappan*, Vol. 80, No. 2 (Oct., 1998), pp. 104–111.

Rosen, Michael: *The Guardian* October 2016.

Shepherd, J.: 'Dividing younger pupils by ability can entrench disadvantage, study finds.' *The Guardian* February 2012

Slavin, R.: *Cooperative Learning*; Boston, MA: Allyn & Bacon 1995.

Vygotsky, L.S.: *Thought and Language*; Boston, MA: MIT Press 1978.

nat drives exceptional teaching and learning

Altitude or speed?

There is a general agreement that all learners, not just the most able, need to experience challenge on a day-to-day basis and develop a range of personal strategies that support their engagement and progress. Much of our work since 2004 has been around what we have called high challenge/low threshold learning, exploring the interaction between what challenge looks like and how we offer that challenge in ways that are accessible to more able students from diverse backgrounds and with various needs. How do we make crossing that threshold into high challenge learning irresistible, and how do we convince learners that what lies beyond that door is the highest possible level of satisfaction and achievement? How we provide support for learners on this journey without compromising or negating that intended and wished-for challenge?

In many ways, effective teaching for the more able is about providing opportunities to make useful mistakes, but this is not the same as creating opportunities to fail. Of course, teachers are expected to scaffold learning, but that isn't simply about taking the difficulty out. On the one hand, we may feel the need to support by focusing on receptive understanding and simplification in order to help learners 'keep up', while in the same breath experiencing the fear that offering 'wait time' in discussions appears to be at odds with the requirement for pace. We may find ourselves chasing the clock by coming to the rescue too quickly, or accepting first responses too readily. We need to recognise that knowledge delivered without uncertainty, without the need for our learners to think, is unlikely to be remembered. More able learners need to be given the opportunity for sustained engagement with a task, to be placed in situations that expose them to ambiguity. And yet, the requirements placed on teachers for clarity in their planning may push them into one-dimensional thinking, where there is no room for doubt or alternatives; where we treat the learning process as a *ladder* to climb step by step from one level to another, rather than a *web* offering unlimited opportunities for individual leaners to progress in directions which they have played a significant part in discovering. In short, how do we plan for student choice and provide spaces for them to think?

Alberto Manguel (2015) says that the essential art of teaching is to recognise that a teacher:

> can help students discover unknown territories, provide them with specialised information, help create for themselves an intellectual discipline, but above all . . . establish for them a space of mental freedom in which they can exercise their imagination and their curiosity, a place in which they can learn to think.

If teachers are reluctant to challenge through offering that *space of mental freedom*, students will tend not to take themselves too seriously. Passivity or an unwillingness to put their heads above the parapet is demonstrated in many ways – a reluctance to question, the expectation of support, or the need to be entertained as payment in advance for effort. On top of this, peer pressure lurks like a sniper just beyond the proffered threshold, so that learners become unwilling to go over the top into a land of risks, uncertainties and mistakes, however useful they might prove to be.

So how can we address all this in the classroom without killing ourselves with over-preparation, or our students with boredom or over-anxiety?

What do we really mean by differentiation?

Differentiation is a central strand in creating high challenge/low threshold learning. How whole class teaching can engage all learners, irrespective of their ability, in challenging and enriching experiences depends largely on how effectively teachers can make differentiation work. Balancing challenge and support in response to meaningful differences between groups or individual students, such as prior learning experience, prior attainment, gender or EAL status and enabling individual learners to steer their own path is much of what makes more able education tick. Kevin Ashton provides a sharp insight into what differentiation means when he says that *the fruit is the point of the tree; the tree is the point of the fruit* (2015). Ashton is talking about how even the most innovative scientists owe much of what they produce to other scientists – *generations are also generators*, he says. We might apply this idea to what happens in the best classrooms. The learner is the fruit of what the teacher generates in the lesson, but what the teacher has caused to happen has in turn been 'fed' by those same students. The tree (teacher) gives life to the fruit; the fruit (the learner) gives life to the tree (the teacher and the curriculum). The relationship between the two is *dynamic*. It's a *process* – not fixed formula. Differentiation is an exploration of how we match and bond the learning environment to the learner's individuality.

Why is differentiation still an area for development?

Our experience is that many teachers feel ill-equipped to talk about differentiation, even those rated as outstanding, perhaps finding it hard to be explicit how differentiation actually works in their classroom. While some aspects of the teachers' craft are more implicit than others it is probably fair to say that there is some confusion over what differentiation is and how it works, both in terms of planning and practice. A key issue is language. Until a school has a consistent language, a way to talk about strategies used to differentiate, then it remains a very complex area to evaluate. Unless there is an agreed common language and key strategies to achieve it, then Art, Maths, Drama, English and PE will never be able to talk to each other in a coherent and purposeful way.

Historically, More Able policies in many schools came down to two broad approaches – which can be (slightly unfairly) summarised as:

1. We set lots of open-ended tasks.
2. There is plenty of extension work for our pupils if they finish the task.

This combination of open-endedness and extension is problematic. If open-endedness means creativity and critical thinking, fine. Otherwise, the first of these is essentially differentiation by outcome, which is simply inevitable. You turn up. So do they. Magic. And the reality is that open-ended tasks can deliver very closed responses. Learning to cope with open-endedness is about teaching or managing learning in more creative ways and this may take some colleagues well away from their comfort zone.

The second can be seen by many students as differentiation by punishment. Teachers setting tasks that reward learners for their arduous work with yet more work, planning this in advance when it may not be used, possibly not having time to assess or even acknowledge it properly, is all pretty pointless. Saving the best or biggest questions until last or providing rewarding and enriching work only to those who cope with the ordinary routine, is concerning.

Guilty until proven innocent?

In some schools, differentiation is quite rigidly planned, with pressure exerted on teachers to prove, way in advance of the lesson, how they will nurture individual leaners. This can involve colleagues taking hours to design tiered tasks, giving students a range of pre-arranged and pre-resourced choices, with extensive opportunities for enrichment. Never mind differentiation by process, this is differentiation by everything, including the kitchen sink, and it is frankly unsustainable. It is also counter-intuitive to what differentiation could mean.

'Less is more' is a useful mantra for how differentiation should work for more able learners, but do all of our colleagues have the confidence or perspective to be able to strip out the chaff, or the willingness to allow learners the freedom to be able to do this for themselves? Why is it the case that differentiation should automatically show up in a lesson plan? When we ask teachers what makes for a really good lesson they often mention learners taking risks, expressing unusual or very personal insights, showing flair or discovering their individual voice as a learner. How do we plan for these?

Top-down planning

A strong message in more able education has been for top-down planning. This has been partly driven by the need to shift colleagues away from more pedestrian, linear teaching and a glib view of differentiation that starts from the average student or 'up a bit, down a bit, left a bit, right a bit' approaches.

The top-down message supports the 'rising tides' argument, which takes the view that with high aspirations for all, we should encourage all learners towards higher achievement. In terms of classroom ethos this is taken as a given, but does the top-down principle always apply?

What higher order thinking (see Glossary) looks like differs according to the age of the learner, the subject, how it is assessed and in other ways which make the hierarchical view of models like Bloom's difficult to sustain (Anderson, Krathwohl, Airasian, Cruikshank, and Mayer, 2000). High performance in maths or science, for example, requires the ability to be able to use small fragments of knowledge or to follow specific processes accurately. What the hierarchy shows in fact are that lower order skills can in practice be very challenging to learn. A more bottom-up approach to planning in these circumstances may well make far more sense. A great deal of recent research, (and ED Hirsch's whole philosophy) is based on giving students essential knowledge as a pre-requisite to understanding and engagement. No easy 'rising tide' metaphors here.

Either way, the teacher's activity can always mask a lack of active engagement by the student. A more useful approach is to consider what the learner is actual being asked to do. From this perspective, another definition of higher order thinking emerges. This involves any activity where learners are required to take a range of inputs (ideas, resources, knowledge, data, etc.) and apply, rearrange and/or extend these to produce their own product (ideas, processes, solutions, analysis). Higher order thinking occurs when learners are *required* to think for themselves, so differentiation in turn relates to how teachers create the conditions for this to happen.

10 ways to think about differentiation

In our work, we have devised a framework called *10 ways to think about differentiation*, which offers a framework for thinking about differentiation through the following approaches:

- Task;
- Resource;
- Assessment;
- Pace (sequence);
- Support;
- Extension;
- Research;
- Dialogue;
- Grouping;
- Self-direction/negotiation.

Task: How do we ensure a healthy balance between open and closed questions/answers?

Here, classroom processes are key. Open questions can in the wrong hands produce extremely closed responses. More able pupils usually require less repetition and with the right tasks, progress can and should be at an individual rate. There needs to be an understanding of how open and closed tasks work, the balance between subject-specific knowledge and skills, and how to encourage higher order rather than lower order thinking.

Resource: How do we offer additional content that supports genuine higher order thinking?

The complexity of selected resources needs to be differentiated to support the same learning objectives or tasks, to allow the same learning activity to be set but also be designed to accommodate a variety of learner needs and abilities. The capacity for abstraction is often highlighted as a key distinguishing factor in terms of ability, but well-structured and open resources should allow all students to engage with this level of thinking.

Assessment: How do we provide a range of assessment methods to gain evidence of challenge?

We need to look at how all forms of assessment – oral, written, non-verbal, presentations – and different levelled mark schemes can be used to support assessment and reduce marking time. When done well, formative assessment encourages interesting dialogue between teachers and students on subject-specific strengths or weaknesses, and about the skills and quality of responses and means of improvement.

Pace/Sequence: How do we assess how much practice is required to achieve mastery of content and skills?

The issues of mastery and of accreditation of prior learning are critical to this form of differentiation. Self-selection encourages independence, so teachers need to focus on whether the starting points involved in responding to a task can be staggered for different students. We believe it is not necessary for all students to follow the same routes through schemes of work and that allowance should be made for more able pupils to start further on, or to miss out stages.

Support: How do we offer support only when it is needed and how do we judge when it can be self-selected?

We need to explore exactly when and how scaffolding is used to support progression and how quickly it needs to be removed to enable more able students to begin to establish their own informed responses and writing styles. The danger is often that scaffolding strategies can actually reduce the likelihood of a more able student formulating their own approaches and can reduce the complexities of response needed for top grades.

Extension: How do we offer challenging extension materials without them being seen as just more work?

In any classroom, there is all too often the danger of saving the best until last, with the most interesting, and challenging issues being held back until everyone is up to speed. The dangers of this are all too obvious, with smart students having to tread water before they can engage in real challenge. Extension tasks done well offer different objectives and task ceilings and allow for far greater flexibility in classwork and more meaningful homework.

Research: How do we best support the skills of active research and offer alternative sources of information?

This explores issues such as what level of independence is required to complete tasks, what variety of sources of information either we or our students use and what method of selection or choice do we use in deciding sources. What we want to do is to develop active research skills that involve our students in the genuine co-construction of learning.

Dialogue: How do we use classroom questions to encourage exploratory talk and active listening?

We need as teachers to effectively balance levels of interaction with or between students (interdependent learning) along with our own use of expert modelling/scaffolding. Differentiated questioning needs to challenge, support and elicit understanding as well as address the balance between teacher and student-generated questioning and feedback. To know how to question is to know how to teach.

Grouping: How do we encourage the social skills students need to capitalise on the freedom of group work?

Just because students are in a group does not mean they are working as a group. We need to experiment with various combinations of students in specific roles, engaging in cooperative learning tasks. These roles in themselves need to be differentiated – the more able students as expert, project manager, or assessor of the debates, which can be also be useful in reducing the isolated social cost of being more able.

Self-direction/negotiation: How do we decide what conditions are required for students to set their own direction?

As teachers, we need to ascertain to what extent self-assessment by students should be used to help them to find their own current level and then allow them to set their own learning objectives/targets. This is often regarded by many schools as by far the most challenging strategy as it can make serious demands on both school time tabling and teacher expertise.

A closer look at tasks and grouping

High challenge can and should be accessible to all learners. Traditional approaches to teaching, CPD and interventions for able learners have tended to focus on how teachers can understand learners' needs and how this understanding informs the support provided, within and beyond the classroom. Many approaches used to support access to a task can do so in a way that may negate the intended challenge. Indeed, by providing this support for learners as part of whole class learning, teachers may unintentionally subvert the challenge for all.

If we were to select for further discussion the two approaches most often cited by schools, they would be task and grouping. Complex rich tasks cover basic areas of learning but also allow for extension far beyond them. Based on genuine exploration, intellectual excitement and challenge, as teachers we need to ensure that the tasks we set in class expand student options. The following key principles for identifying and setting richer and more complex tasks should help to make the tasks and activities set more stimulating for all students, but genuinely more challenging for the more able.

I. 'Richer' tasks

Rich tasks should develop from a common core of knowledge or skills, generally one that would be covered by the class within their normal working day. The rich task provides for this basic level of learning but also offers opportunities for learners to move far beyond it. The challenge is to take these common classroom tasks and enrich them. The core will generally encompass an element of subject material that the class needs to learn about or learn to do. Socratic talk (see Glossary) should be used to enable learners to elicit understanding, explore the meaning within the task and how it offers potential for learning. Depending on what they are used to, this may require some negotiation.

They should also encourage genuine exploration of a topic with an element of open-endedness.

Tasks might encourage learners to explore the subject material, rather than merely provide an answer or complete a closely defined set task. This does not mean that there is no right solution or end product – rather, that there will be a range of them. There may be an initial, well-defined task that all learners will be expected to achieve and then students are encouraged to move on to more open-ended tasks, or the entire task may allow a wide range of possible responses. There is generally no 'set' way of answering at least part of the task – learners will approach the task differently depending on how they learn and their current levels of knowledge and ability.

A rich task generally enables learners to think and act 'in role.' Whether this is as a mathematician, scientist or writer, they support the development of authentic expertise on the part of the student, to explore a context from a particular perspective and to produce responses which enable them to develop their voice as a potential or emergent expert. Joseph Renzulli talks about *type 3* enrichment as the most stretching, and by this he means the use of real world problems faced by people working in the field (2015). For many of us, this is the wider objective of more able education: expertise in development, solving genuine problems.

Learners come to tasks from a wide range of backgrounds – some may have in-depth knowledge of a subject while others may have minimal knowledge; some will be interested, some not so keen. A well-planned rich task will allow for this, providing a range of choices that cater for all levels and abilities. By the end of a task all of the learners should have fulfilled the core requirement, while some of the learners will have gone far beyond this. To allow this to happen learners must be enabled to engage with a wide range of start and end points that allow for a wide continuum of responses.

The more open-ended nature of rich tasks will provide opportunities for higher-level thinking, if the classroom environment supports this approach. If teachers comment positively on work that goes beyond the bare minimum and are interested in different approaches to tasks, then learners will feel encouraged and supported in responding to rich tasks to the best of their ability. In a tightly constrained class, where there is one 'right' answer and the teacher is the only authority, learners will focus on providing what they feel the teacher is looking for, which inevitably limits the richness of responses.

Rich tasks will ask learners to analyse, synthesise and/or evaluate in the course of completing the task. Rich tasks are not about simple recall of facts or repetition of learned procedures; they require higher-level cognitive processing. Facts and procedures may be the starting point for some rich tasks, but they are not the end point. Rich tasks encourage learners to think creatively, work logically, synthesise their results, analyse disparate viewpoints, look for common features or evaluate findings. This is not to say that rich tasks might not also include lower-level activities, but this knowledge will have arisen from or be activated by a process of questioning and enquiry.

Creativity is strongly linked to higher ability and rich tasks give learners permission to be more creative in their responses. As with higher-level thinking, the level of creativity will also depend on the nature of the classroom – in a tightly constrained classroom, learners may not feel that creativity is either allowed or welcomed. Rich tasks also enable learners to appreciate the value of variety and differences in perspective – a really good example will also enable learners to see elements of beauty in a context, an elegant solution or the imaginative use of humour.

An element of choice, both in task and in end product, allows learners to work to their strengths and interests. Choices should be varied to ensure that learners encounter a wide range of tasks and products over the course of the school year. If we look at just the synthesis level of Bloom's taxonomy, this will mean that learners may be asked to arrange, compose, construct, design, develop, formulate, plan, prepare, propose, set up or write. So, the end product could be written or oral, a model or a PowerPoint presentation, an interview or a debate, allowing for a range of methods of assessment. Choices allow learners to feel ownership of the task or tasks and research consistently shows that this, in turn, will increase their level of effort, engagement and enjoyment.

The range of choice and challenge in rich tasks make them inherently more interesting to learners. Tightly constrained tasks with a set endpoint tend to allow the learners no individuality in either their approach or their output. All correct answers to fixed questions tend to be similar. The interest is in the end product or solution, with little or no interest in the process for getting there. In a rich task, learners have choices to make. Teachers will be interested in how they arrived at their chosen endpoint and why they made the choices they did. All of this makes the rich tasks more interesting for both the student and the teacher.

The open-ended nature and high level of challenge in more complex tasks provide opportunities for learners to show what they are capable of achieving. Such tasks can therefore help in identifying able or gifted learners, particularly those who are 'hidden' or unidentified. They also allow a finer-grained analysis of individual strengths and weaknesses than tightly constrained tasks, linking to assessment for learning strategies. These tasks enable learners to produce different kinds of products, to present their learning in a variety of ways and to be assessed at the level of their potential as well as their current attainment.

2. Differentiation through grouping

Teachers group pupils in several ways: by comparable ability, by mixed ability, by friendship, by gender, by personality and randomly. Some use groups for some of the time; others for all of the time. Some maintain the same groupings; others vary the group according to the task or the subject. Grouping pupils within the class can enable resources to be shared and can foster social development. The fact, however, that pupils are seated in groups does not necessarily mean that they are working as a group. Group work may quickly become counter-productive if teachers try too many groups or have pupils working on too many different activities or subjects simultaneously, but when it is done well it is a very powerful differentiation tool. There is considerable research to show that as much thinking and learning occurs *between* students as happen *within* students.

There are a couple of phrases used by psychologists which emphasise the importance of the grouping process: *secondary intersubjectivity* and *social referencing*. It's partly about turning to someone else in the room for interpretative help, but it's also about how working in groups helps learners to make use and build on what we would argue are the crucial elements of mystery, difficulty, uncertainty and even anxiety that they meet as part of their learning.

Collaborative or co-operative group work

Although these terms are often used interchangeably, a helpful distinction can be made. Collaborative work is shared by two or more pupils whose design, planning and/or materials and so on are left to the group to decide. The outcomes of collaborative work are likely to be open-ended – original, idiosyncratic even. Co-operative work is shared by two or more pupils where the task and/or resources and possibly the children's roles are specified by the teacher. The outcomes are likely to be what the teacher expects. Both have a place. In terms of co-operative learning, it is essential to establish how students will acquire the skills they need to be effective group members, including exploring what impact differences in tasks have on group talk, what opportunities learners have to talk about their own activity *and* comment on others, and the extent to which students are encouraged to help each other to complete individual tasks. In terms of collaborative learning it's that phrase, *space of mental freedom* again, where learners have ultimate control over methodology, pace and the ultimate destination of the pathways they are choosing to take.

Other significant issues to consider include why children are grouped in a particular way, what are the advantages and disadvantages of grouping in any of these different ways, (according to gender, or ability for instance) how to plan the division of time between the different groups, whether the groups are fixed or dynamic and critically, if the grouping is appropriate to the learning intention?

Grouping strategies

The following might reward exploration:

Cascade: One or more children learn or develop a skill, knowledge or understanding and are then required to 'pass this learning on' to one or more children.

Paired Tutoring: A 'one-stage' version of cascade where a 'more advanced' child is paired with a 'less advanced' child in order to help develop their learning.

Envoy: Different groups work on different parts of the same task or on different tasks. At a given signal, one from each group (the 'envoy') is sent to another group to report on their group's findings or ideas.

Goldfish: Effective for tasks that can be divided up and that focus on sequenced parts, for example, a study of consecutive paragraphs of a text, or of the stages of a process in science or geography. Each group is allocated a different part of the task to discuss or investigate, perhaps one paragraph or stage. At a given signal, each group's findings are passed on in some form to the group studying the next part in the sequence (for example orally by one member of each group, or as a diagram or written account provided by the group). The new group studies and discusses the new information.

Carousel/country dance: Equal numbers of children sit in an inner and outer circle (A and B), facing each other. Each child in one circle speaks to its partner, sharing new information, expressing ideas or rehearsing arguments. At a signal, the children in the other circle take a turn at doing the same while their partners listen.

Snowball: Children may work individually to start with. If so, at a signal after a while they are paired together and compare notes, collate their findings or negotiate on their task finding in some way. At another signal, pairs join into fours and repeat the exercise. If desired, at another signal, fours join to become eights and repeat. (Turn-taking and/or negotiation techniques in the groups need to be modelled and practised so that this works effectively.)

Jigsaw: Especially suited to 'body of knowledge' learning. Each child within initial groups of 5 or 6 is given a number or a name. These re-form as groups of children with the same number or name, as 'expert groups'. Expert groups are allocated different pieces of research or investigations to undertake (groups may usefully be split into pairs, then the pairs may collate their findings with other pairs in the expert group). After this, children return to their initial ('home') groups as the experts in their field and are required to report their findings to these groups. (They may need support in presenting findings and/or taking turns within home groups.)

Pair swapping: Pairs work together on a task (this task may be the same, or different pairs). On a signal from the teacher, one from each pair is swapped with another, and required to report on what they have done or to 'add' their learning to that of their new partner in some way. This makes it difficult for unmotivated underachievers to 'coast' through a whole session. Pair work may also be less threatening than larger group work.

Pupils as teachers: Groups are set up to design interesting ways to deliver various subject based topics – selecting effective ways to resource, research and present their chosen topic. They are given time to produce a variety of teaching packs, including videos, booklets and games, which they can present before a class/teachers/parents/invited audience.

The above is not an exhaustive list of grouping strategies, but we have found them all to be very effective in widely different environments and with different cohorts of ability. When used thoughtfully, with clear intent and with the issues above fully considered, we have observed on many occasions that such strategies can be highly effective tools in the teacher's armoury to support and develop the use of differentiation, particularly for the more able student.

Other ways of seeing differentiation

The truth is that there are, in fact, *more* than 'ten ways' of looking at differentiation. There are others that can be used equally effectively. Moving in clear steps from the concrete to the abstract, for instance. Thinking in the abstract is a crucial element in developing originality and learners need to be able to manipulate abstract ideas and to use them flexibility within and between subjects. This is not rocket science – abstract thinking can be as simple as learners suggesting rules that they can then use to make further deductions.

In a similar way, moving from the simple to the more complex is also powerful. It is often said that more able students require tasks that are more complex in resources, research, issues, problems, skills, or goals than less advanced peers. However, simplification is a skill in itself, and an important test of a more able child is their ability to be able to précis ideas and argument.

The move from basic to transformational is essentially a way to make new thinking out of old – making sure that the learner is required to think for themselves, which usually involves producing something that is not the same as what they were given (see Glossary on transforming *déjà vu* to *vuja de*). This can often be achieved by going from fewer facets of a concept to exploring multiple facets. Learners need to be given meaningful choices in their learning – creating questions and hypotheses to explain increasingly complex ideas, spotting patterns and testing their ideas to see if they work.

Learners advanced in a subject often benefit from tasks that require greater mental leaps in insight, application, or transfer than less advanced peers. As discussed above, scaffolding-out challenge is one of the greatest dangers in task design. Therefore, moving from the more structured to greater openness in tasks in regard to solutions and decisions, can be powerful.

Greater independence in planning, designing, and self-monitoring can also work. But being able to learn with others – interdependence – is in many ways the most important aspect for more able learners, so in this case independence really means ownership, giving learners more control of the task, to self-direct or to be free to negotiate the meaning and scope of a task for themselves.

Can differentiation work?

We mention elsewhere that the former head of the UK's inspection process made the point that effective differentiation is *hugely difficult*. He maintains that we have confused honing good classroom practice with social engineering. We have put an ambition to make sure everyone has access to the same learning experiences above individual needs and potential. Attempting to teach mixed-ability classes doesn't work, he says, unless there is mixed-ability teaching – a clear sense, in other words, of what differentiation is and how it works in the classroom. If all of this seems like hard work, it really does not have to be. Responding to individuals is simply about showing interest, reflecting their own questions back to them, taking an active and questioning interest in activities and, at the end of such a process, using leading questions to encourage further thinking.

The painter Francis Bacon said that, *it is the artist's job the deepen the mystery* (2013). We would argue that this is the teacher's job too but that it can only happen when what learners encounter in the classroom arouses interest, challenges, intrigues, stimulates curiosity; where the resources they are offered have the potential to 'take them to the edges' of their capacity to understand; where teaching responds to where they are as individuals in terms of their own development (as opposed to where they stand in relation to their peers) and allows for variations in pace – sometimes fast, sometimes slow.

In short, differentiation need not be *hugely difficult*. Simply repeat: the fruit is the point of the tree; the tree is the point of the fruit. Focus on the individuals in the classroom and remember that the more your work is student-driven, responsive to variations in pace and open to a whole variety of potential pathways, then the more successful those students will be – as individuals, in their exams and in their future lives.

References

Anderson, L., Krathwohl, D., Airasian, P., Cruikshank, A., and Mayer, R.: *A Taxonomy for Learning, Teaching, and Assessing: A Revision of Bloom's Taxonomy of Educational Objectives*; London: Pearson 2000.

Ashton, K.: *How to Fly a Horse: The Secret History of Creation, Invention and Discovery*; London: Heinemann 2015.

Bacon, F.: 'The Job of the Artist' Available at: www.artsy.net/article/christies-francis-bacon-on-the-job-of-the-artist.

Bonawitz, E., Shafto, P., Gweon, H., Goodman, N.D., Spelke, E., and Schulz, L.: 'The double edged sword of pedagogy: Instruction limits spontaneous exploration and discovery'; *Cognition* 2011.

Dweck, C.S.: *Self-theories: their role in Motivation, Personality and Development*; Abingdon, UK: Psychology Press 1999.

Graham, J.: *Ink*; London: Bloomsbury Methuen, 2017.

Manguel, A.: *Curiosity*; New Haven: Yale 2015.

Renzulli, J. et al.: *Reflections on Gifted Education*; London: Prufrock 2015.

Weale, Sally: 'Moderate anxiety may contribute to academic attainment in school'; *The Guardian* July 2017.

Chapter 10

Dependence to independence
Autopilot or co-pilot?

If you treat people as they are, you will be instrumental in keeping them as they are. If you treat them as they could be, you will help them become what they ought to be.

(Goethe, 2013)

Enabling learners to take themselves more seriously as students

It is hard for students to take responsibility when they are sometimes given so few opportunities in school to exercise any. They become trapped in a 'locus of control' cameo role. They don't see themselves as independent reflective individuals, but more passive receivers of the teacher's wisdom. It's not how much effort they put in that matters, but whether they get the right notes given to them to conveniently regurgitate at the right time. How can we encourage our students to take more responsibility for their own learning and what can we do that will help to make risk-taking paradoxically a safer option in our classrooms? In the current situation, what's their incentive to change? The less they do, the more we do on their behalf. They get their thinking done for them by us, and then handed back out to them on a bite-sized platter. It's no wonder they so often complain of boredom.

Addressing the issues of 'learned helplessness'

When we asked a group of highly successful headteachers what they thought independence looked like they came up with the following:

Focused
Determined/persistent
Self-motivated
Able to work on his/her own
Completes homework
Able to follow instructions
Meets deadlines
Meets targets
Acts on advice
Doesn't waste time

It is important to make the distinction between someone who can work well on his/her own and genuine independence. The list above tends to represent what the Heads wanted in their school. Compliance. Behind this idea is the premise that we can *teach* 'executive control', we can show learners how to develop self-discipline so that they can focus, control their behaviour and persevere. Most teachers would say that students to have self-discipline is a vital component if we are to achieve the hoped-for academic outcomes. Angela Duckworth's notion of grit promotes the idea that we can release teacher executive control, and goes to great lengths to show us how this might happen – in families and in classrooms (see Glossary). This kind of learner might be the 'top grades across the board' high achiever, but even so they may well not be being prepared effectively for the kind of future that awaits them beyond the requirements of the next test. Paradoxically, the Duckworth approach suggests that self-control can be imposed by others from the outside. Bonawitz and colleagues talk about '*the double-edged sword of pedagogy*' where instruction can limit, or drown out, the development of autonomy (2011). This is not to say that promoting self-discipline is wrong and encouraging autonomy is right. They are two sides of the same coin – autonomy needs self-control; self-control develops through increasing autonomy. We need to give learners the time to find that balance.

Are schools too careless with, or too reliant on, '*the sword of pedagogy*'? There is little doubt that we can sometimes undermine our own best intentions. In the second *Austin Powers* film, before Dr. Evil was sent back in time to 1969, his minions made him a clone. The clone was identical to him in every way but was 'one-eighth his size'. Upon being introduced to his clone, Dr. Evil immediately declared, '*Breathtaking. I shall call him . . . Mini-Me*'. Later in the film he adds, '*Mini-Me, you complete me*'. It is hard as a teacher not to take on board responsibilities for our students, to help them to develop as experts, to take them under our collective wings and help them fly. But we sometimes fly too close to them, and are reluctant to address their mistakes or their laziness. The problem with Mini-Mes is that they just aren't that successful in the long run.

There needs to be a substantial transfer of accountability between adults and students. In James Graham's play, *Ink*, set in the Fleet Street of 1969, he has a tabloid editor, Hugh Cudlipp, say: *Pander and promote the most base instincts of people all you like, fine, create an appetite, but I warn you. You'll have to keep feeding it.* The 'base instincts' we're talking about in relation to learning are those of passivity, an absence of seriousness about learning, and an expectation that learning will be always easy and entertaining. We run the risk of pandering to an avoidance of challenge by spoon-feeding or by thinking we must entertain in return for attention. Once on this path we have to shout louder and louder to get that attention, so much so that our teaching becomes an echo chamber where alternative approaches and questions aren't heard and where individual identities are forced into hiding by peer group pressure. Accountability isn't a one-way street and learners and adults have to feel that they share an equal responsibility for what happens through the learning process.

What are some characteristics of more able but dependent students?

Many hundreds of observations of lessons combined with discussions with schools have made it clear that there are serious concerns regarding the level of engagement that students often have with high challenge. One of the most significant factors has emerged as a kind of 'learned helplessness' often demonstrated by students, which is characterised by a dependent attitude, and a lack of initiative. This tends to reveal itself in one of the following ways for More Able but Dependent (MAD) students.

They tend not to take themselves seriously as learners.

They often pretend to be bored or tired to avoid having to engage with difficulty. They tend not to talk back to, negotiate with, or question teachers and assume the teacher's job is to always be on hand with answers. They don't really listen to or value each other's views or ideas and often don't take notes unless directed to do so. They are locked into patterns of underachievement and don't know how to get out of their rut. They don't how to 'customise' their approach to whatever environment they are in and find it difficult to actively manage intellectual interactions.

They don't seem to be interested in becoming expert.

They won't read around the subject unless specifically directed to do so. They often stick rigidly to the demands of the syllabus only, and question teachers who stray off the path. They read Examiners Reports as if they had come down from the Mount and are more worried about how they will be assessed than how they can become more expert in the subject. They offer generalities and opinions without feeling the need to justify or support their answers or opinions. They don't value speculation or intriguing questions, just facts and answers, and are more interested in their mark or result than any explanations or suggestions for deeper learning that their teachers may offer.

They are fearful of being seen as less than smart.

They are often in awe of those students they perceive to be more successful than they are and are dismissive of those who fail. They tend to allow peer pressure to overly influence them. They are reluctant to move out of their familiar language base or to use adventurous or speculative language. They show reluctance in demonstrating learning and knowledge in debates, in case they might be wrong and often don't see themselves or their ideas as being worthy of adult attention and interest.

They don't choose to take risks or go outside their comfort zones.

They shirk taking responsibilities and new opportunities for learning. They are rarely subversive or irreverent in their responses and in turn expect to be supported not challenged, anticipating being entertained or indulged in lessons. They are more content with exposition and stories than analysis, which they often claim to be too dry, and so they rarely choose to engage with real complexity. They don't really learn a sense of confidence, entitlement and adventure; instead they tend to learn uncertainty, constraint and caution.

The additional dangers of dependency

A good example of the dangers of unsuccessful student learning strategies was well illustrated in the famous experiment by Professor Carol Dweck when she gave a class of high school girls workbooks to complete, some of them containing a set of extra questions that were above the girls' current level of attainment. The girls not given the inserts performed normally on the test, but for the others the normal pattern of high and low achievement was actually reversed. The bright girls, who usually coasted along, panicked when they came up against the unknown – their confidence, based on the idea that they were 'clever' crumbled when they didn't automatically know the answers.

This does not mean that we should not raise the level of challenge, rather that we should enable our students to deal with difficult tasks with a different mindset. Dweck acknowledges that by creating scaffolds that can effectively remove the challenge, we are not equipping our students to know what strategies they can use when they are confronted with hard tasks. She went on to add that:

> It doesn't help a child to tackle a difficult task if they succeed constantly on an easy one. It doesn't teach them to persist in the face of obstacles if obstacles are always eliminated. . . . [W]hat children learn best from are slightly difficult tasks which they have to struggle through. Knowing they can cope with difficulties is what makes children seek challenges and overcome further problems.
>
> (1999)

This very usefully raises the issue of praise and suggests that raising effort is far more effective than praising intelligence. Other educators such as Alfie Kohn argue that all praise should be separated from feedback. There are clear dangers of gratuitous praise as students can immediately feel patronised. They may also feel that the activity itself is being devalued as simply a means to an end (successful completion rather than learning). Kohn suggests '*process praise*' should be given, not on individual effort, but rather on what has been produced (1999). This includes praising the kind of struggles that students have gone through.

What level of independence should schools be seeking?

An independent learner needs to be much more than someone who works well on his or her own. They need to be a confident, social individual who learns at least as well with and from their peers, as they do from the teacher, or on their own. This raises questions for the ways that we set up our classrooms, some of which are likely to be:

How can we encourage our students to become less dependent?
What does it mean to take risks in learning?
How do we encourage learners in our class to be less fearful?
How can we enable learners to make useful mistakes?
What might a whole school approach on independence look like?

The issues of MAD students highlighted above have led us to a focus on what skills we want our learners to develop that will enable them to be better equipped for the complex and uncertain demands of the current century. In these times, alliteration is all. So we looked at grouping the skills under the headings of strategic, social and speculative learners, although frankly it would have been possible to come up with a variety of different classifications. What actually matters is that this (or a similar set of skills) are agreed across your school as being appropriate for your learners.

Once we have looked at and decided on some of the behaviours and skills that we would wish all of our students to develop, the next big leap is to look at how we can address the issues of student dependency in relation to them.

What are the characteristics of successful learners?

Table 10.1

Strategic	Social	Speculative
Independent	Interdependent	Inventive
Reflective	Responsive	Curious
Evaluative	Intuitive	Risk taking
Adaptable	Collaborative	Experimental
Logical	Active	Inquisitive
Responsible	Self-aware	Observant
Determined	Receptive	Questioning

If we agree that we want our learners to see themselves as, for example, strategic, speculative and social learners, how can we help them to develop those skills, with a focus on creating more independent learning situations in our classrooms?

The thinking below is a way of mapping what we would want our students to become and ways we believe will help to encourage it. We look at each aspect of independence, focusing on ways that we can convince students to live their aspirations.

How to encourage social independence

As a teacher and learner, talk about your own learning histories, particularly when you struggled to understand. Learn aloud and externalise your thinking, feelings and decision-making so that your students can follow the processes and understand the difficulties involved. One of the most important lessons young people can learn is that they are not alone.

Have visible, ongoing, speculative learning projects focused on things that there might not be easy answers to in your subject. Ask them to discuss and contribute their own thoughts and intuitions to these projects.

Focus on quality of response, brevity and tight timelines but try not to become the ringmaster. Allow your students opportunities to lead sections of the lesson, including plenary sessions. Don't just reward the fast thinkers in discussions; approaches such as 'think, pair, share,' give your students collaboration, exploration and reassurance time.

Don't accept their first easy or glib soundbite responses and instead rigorously use 'so what' interrogation approaches to challenge selected students to go beyond the superficial. They need to become more aware of what they are capable of thinking, but also why they think these things and how they can justify them. Provide specific opportunities for able pupils to show what they can achieve. Be prepared to negotiate, to be surprised or to be wrong.

However tempting it is, try not to paraphrase on their behalf. Before your students are allowed to speak in debates, sometimes insist that they accurately paraphrase the previous speaker and demonstrate how the point they will be making follows on from what has gone before. This means that they need to be genuinely responsive to their classmates, rather than just waiting until they have finished before launching into a new opinion.

How to encourage speculative independence

Actively encourage your students to chew over, digest and question your learning methods. This encourages a clearer understanding of what you are trying to do and what you expect/want from them.

Present your students with subject matter that is genuinely difficult and therefore more intriguing. Try to not pre-empt their learning by pre-chewing the materials and 'neatening up' the learning process. Be perfectly prepared to pull away the rug to challenge their sense of security. Your students can also only really learn to become more experimental if you yourself are prepared to take risks and fail.

Respond to unforeseen events and questions in your lesson in ways that model curiosity and learning to your students. Try to make your learning environment a safe place to be uncertain and to make mistakes. Use probing questions to deepen the level of challenge. Be open about your responses when you are asked genuinely challenging questions.

Encourage your students to meet ideas with a 'could be' point of view and genuine questions. Establish that the significant questions in your subject have a wide number of possible solutions and that easy facts are often convenient simplifications.

Wait before you reveal the purpose/objective of your lesson. Give your students the chance to be inquisitive before it gets too locked down too soon. Rather than restricting potential exploration at the outset give your students a chance to discover their own limits or methods. By not trying to control or regulate how they approach tasks or where they are going with them, you might be surprised by where their journeys can take your lessons. Give yourself time in the lesson to observe what is happening and to give the students thinking space. Allow them time to observe and comment on the lesson to improve their own noticing abilities.

Try not to support their helplessness by reassuring/intervening when they encounter a block. Allow your students to struggle and not get it, and then have to work out ways to get it for themselves. Don't fall into the controlling trap of thinking you always need to be there to support or scaffold out difficulty. Setting up protocols like 'three before me' lets your students know they must go elsewhere for ideas and that you are not ambulatory Google on tap. Your students need to be allowed/enabled to form their own ideas and to learn from their mistakes. Only by experiencing key blocks to their learning and overcoming them can your students learn how they learn, and develop the necessary strategies they will need later in their lives.

Don't unconsciously prejudge outcomes or define the parameters of inquiry. Often it is only by letting your students off the lead that you will find out what they are capable of achieving. Try not to leave the best/most challenging activities to last where time is often tight and discussion usually rushed. Don't always require a detailed written response. Having built-in writing free days/weeks and using thinking maps as evidence of inquiry allows students more freedom to explore.

Encouraging strategic independence

To begin with, it is probably a smart move to let your students understand your high expectations of them through the tasks that you set, and the language that you use. Using complex and technical vocabulary helps them to start to think and express themselves with the precision necessary to eventually see themselves or start to become scientists/linguists/historians. Be really specific about what you require your students to do in an activity and don't backtrack if they initially resist or complain. What you believe they can achieve can have a significant impact on their motivation. Keep your ambitions on their behalf high and make your expectations and their responsibilities clear.

Keep reminding your students to focus on what their learning priorities are, in terms of their own learning journey. Encourage them to compare their past and present results, which can start to form the basis of a focused discussion. Ensure that they know how each activity can contribute to their learning, where they can take it next and how they can evaluate it themselves.

Clarify that consistently achieving top marks is easy success and really just means that the challenge was insufficient; it is only through increased effort and determination that they will really achieve. Show them that finding things pretty difficult is a significant part of the learning process and that encountering difficulty is actually where they start to learn.

On occasion take your students 'behind the curtain' of your lesson to help them to access and understand your teaching and learning intentions. If the lesson needs to be adapted during class discussions and veers away from where it was going, let the students know why that shift is often a significant learning moment. Have an element of choice (either in the task or in the response) built into the lesson, allowing students to exercise self-direction. Allow them to exercise critical autonomy. Take their views seriously enough to interrogate and scrutinise them.

Encourage students to understand the benefits of peer assessments and the importance of reflecting on their own and others' achievements. Students should get used to being their own first marker and editor, and once they are doing that successfully they should be encouraged to work in collective groups to mark and evaluate one another's work.

Don't be afraid to set high challenge beyond syllabus tasks and don't allow the specifications to define the learning; even though that may be a tough call it is necessary one, especially if you want to explore the genuinely interesting aspects of your subject that might encourage your students to want to take it further.

Desirable difficulties as a whole school approach

How can we avoid the dangers of being positioned as our students' 'life support machines', keeping them going for as long as possible, with the only measurable output from them on their own behalf being a pulse? Or becoming the even more familiar 'knights in shining armour,' dashing to their rescue way before there is any distress expressed, in order to keep them 'on track' and to make sure they don't feel uncomfortable or get demotivated. And we have all allowed ourselves at some point to become the 'echo chamber' happily over praising and paraphrasing students' comments for the others who weren't listening and helpfully adding a little rigour too. We have often become accustomed to accepting our students' first sound bite responses too readily, not planning spaces for them to think and not properly grilling their responses. And our students know all of this. We need to remind ourselves that lessons are not echo chambers that give back to students what they want and expect; they should be places of reasoned, rational debate and conversation.

So what's their incentive to change? The less they do, the more we do on their behalf. They get their thinking done for them and then handed out to them on a platter. It's no wonder they so often complain of stifling boredom.

Perhaps intuitively we believe that we can speed up the learning process by making the information that we give our students as simple as possible, and with effective scaffolding in place. More able learners need to be given the opportunity for sustained engagement with a task, to be placed in situations that expose them to ambiguity, yet the requirements for clarity in planning may limit opportunities for doubt. We need to plan for greater student choice and provide spaces for them to think and to struggle.

Robert Bjork believes that current performance is an unhelpful proxy for learning, particularly with regard to the likelihood of retention and transfer. He advocates introducing 'desirable difficulties' as these have a positive impact on our ability to transfer information to different fields and improve our mastery of the information. He argues that introducing variability and difficulty into teaching slows down performance but increases long-term retention. For an overview of Robert Bjork and the concept see 'Desirable difficulties in the classroom' (2011). This clearly makes a mockery of what OFSTED seek in terms of rapid progress in every lesson. Some of the desirable difficulties make a great deal of sense. The idea that we should give clues rather than offer a complete solution puts the learner back at the heart of the process of learning. They have to work harder to process the material and that makes it easier to transfer from working to long-term memory. The idea of introducing variety, ambiguity and unpredictability into our classrooms means that our students can't relax, and they need to concentrate and pay attention. It introduces necessary struggle. We cannot continue to be supportive cheerleaders of their self-esteem and we cannot always protect them from some anxiety – as Frederic N Bierce says: *students may be at optimal disposition to succeed in school when they experience moderate levels of anxiety* (qtd. in Weale 2017).

Final thoughts on independence

Now, as teachers we know that there are many interesting and varied ways to self-destruct. We see it in our students but are less inclined to see it in our colleagues or ourselves. But teachers do the professional guilt thing on a regular, self-flagellatory basis better than most other professions.

Critically it must be highlighted that the approaches outlined earlier need to be part of a much **wider school priority** to work effectively. Pushing back against students demands for more and more comprehensive revision notes, refusing to mark anything less than their best work will inevitably cause friction. Our students want an easy time. Often so do we. If any one teacher attempts to do this on his or her own they will quickly become what Trekkies refer to as 'Lieutenant Expendable'. The one viewers have never seen before, first to be sent down from the star-ship to a hostile planet. The one who wears the different-coloured shirt. The one who won't make it back to the Enterprise.

Schools can be cruel and hostile places. The learners within any school can be even more dangerous. If a teacher goes out on a limb by insisting that they won't answer questions, that they will seek to use Socratic dialogue, they will not be endlessly on tap, they will let their learners struggle, and they will certainly not spoon feed, then unsurprisingly their students will often react badly. They will question that teacher's subject knowledge (is that because you don't know the answer, sir?). They will question that teacher's competence (why do other teachers prepare us better for the exam, miss?). They will even question that teacher's motivation (do you really not care about us enough to give us the answers?).

They will do so because they will resent the removal of the easy and contented life they had before, where teachers were always available as the only 'necessary expert', where learners just needed to turn up (and sometimes listen, but hey it would usually be repeated or handed out if you didn't) and where teachers were quite often the source of the main classroom entertainment. They will resent being required to suddenly think for themselves, research independently and commit serious effort into their own understanding. And they will try to take it out on you.

If your school is moving forward with this as a whole, or in a secondary school, if a department decides to take it on, or if a particular year group is targeted, then the process becomes much easier and safer to trial. And it **is** worth implementing for many reasons.

It will in the long run ensure that your learners become committed to their own learning, not just committed to responding in order to get you off their back. It will take away a great deal of stress and pressure that currently resides with you to ensure 'coverage' and progress. It will mean that you have more breathing space in your lessons to actually plan where you want to take things next. But most importantly, it will equip your students with some of the skills they will require for the rest of their lives. And quite frankly, your school is a **far** safer place to learn these skills than anywhere else your learners are likely to find themselves.

Without any doubt, they will **not** receive the support and thoughtfulness that they so take for granted, in either universities or the workplace. Lecturers are often far more concerned with their own research to be duly or unduly worried about individual students who don't seem to be prepared for higher education. Even if they wanted to, it is pretty difficult to personalise learning effectively and to offer support in a lecture hall where there are several hundred others. Employers aren't that keen to engage with whether a student is waving or drowning, if they get it or not. If we don't equip our students with these skills before they leave our schools, they **will** seriously struggle in the longer term.

References

Bye, J.: 'Desirable difficulties in the classroom' *Psychology in Action* 2011. Available at www.psychologyinaction.org/psychology-in-action-1/2011/01/04/desirable-difficulties-in-the-classroom.

Bonawitz, E., et al.: 'The double edged sword of pedagogy: Instruction limits spontaneous exploration and discovery'; *Cognition* 2011.

Dweck, C.S.: *Self-theories: their role in Motivation, Personality and Development*; Abingdon, UK: Psychology Press 1999.

Goethe, Johann: *Wilhelm Meister's Apprenticeship; A Novel*; TheClassics.us 2013.

Graham, J.: *Ink*; London: Bloomsbury Methuen 2017.

Kohn, A.: *Punished by Rewards: The Trouble with Gold Stars, Incentive Plans, A's, Praise, and Other Bribes*; Orlando, FL: Mariner Books 1999.

Roach, J.: *Austin Powers: The Spy Who Shagged Me*; 1999.

Weale, Sally: 'Moderate anxiety may contribute to academic attainment in school'; *The Guardian* July 2017.

Vygotsky, L.: *Mind in Society: The Development of Higher Psychological Processes*; (1962) Harvard revised edition 1978.

Chapter 11

Underachievement and motivation
Lost horizons?

Given that the word, 'traits' carries with it tainted ideas about racial, economic and social supremacy, we replaced it with the word *inclinations* when talking about how some students lean towards one body of knowledge rather than another, or one way of learning as opposed to another. For inclination, we might use the word, motivation. This chapter is about *disinclinations*, missing motivation. In the next chapter, we will consider the need to recognise *disadvantage*, by which we mean those social and economic challenges which make an unfettered engagement with the business of education difficult for many students, the schools they attend and their families. But first we need to look at potentially able students who do not want to achieve. For these students this resistance to, or withdrawal from, the learning and achieving process, is not about that student's background community but rather a *disinclination* to learn that does not emerge from the beliefs and expectations of that student's background. The barriers to achievement come about because they have effectively built *a wall in the head* against a serious engagement with learning (Hanley, 2007).

This chapter is about that *disinclination* to engage, about understanding the state of mind that effectively builds Lynsey Hanley's *wall in the head*, and how we might convert resistance into interest and commitment. The wall may have been constructed with bricks made of troubling social or cultural issues, but equally it could be about gender, personality, classroom experiences, relationships, emotional or behavioural factors, boredom, curricular issues or unrecognised learning disabilities. Although school will almost certainly be the place where the underachievement shows itself most clearly, and although school is not the *only* place where its causes need to be addressed and overcome, we really do need to believe that the way we organise and think about our work, and the way we interact with students in the classroom, can lower the wall, if not knock it down altogether.

In the chapter on community disadvantage we describe a self-review process that might help us to root out those external factors that limit learning and engagement. Before that we want to look more closely at the individual and some of those 'symptoms' of underachievement that might help us to recognise who we are talking about and begin to think through how we might respond (Karaduman, 2013). In our classrooms, have we met, for instance: the individual who responds well one-to-one, but is aimless when working independently; one who is a slow starter or an ineffective finisher; or a poor listener ('What was it you said we had to do?'); likes attention and is easily distracted without attention; complains about peers ('Miss, tell him!'); is often moody; demanding – and is disorganised – no pen, no books, no PE kit. Reis and McCoach

(2000), help us to categorise, or spot the symptoms, in this list of other pointers to the whys and wherefores of underachievement:

1. *Personality characteristics* – low self-esteem, immaturity, dependence and a lack of resilience.
2. *Internal mediators* – fear of failure or success, like Carol Dweck's idea that able children may fear being 'caught out' as less able; an individual who externalises problems, is negative, antisocial or rebellious, or conversely, a perfectionist.
3. *Differential Thinking Skills or Styles* – impatient with – detailed thinking (or the reverse), and with repetition.
4. *Maladaptive Strategies* – Poor goal-setting, coping strategies, self-regulation, perseverance, self-control – and is defensive.
5. *Positive Qualities* – intense interest beyond the curriculum; creative; rejects unchallenging work with a lack of tact.

An analysis by Mandel and Marcus (1988) goes further and gives us, we think, a more than recognisable list of the types of underachievers we have almost all certainly met:

- *Coasting types*: contented procrastinators who sound sincere but do not deliver.
- *Anxious types*: tense, uptight, self-critical, self-doubting.
- *Defiant*: often a 'boy thing': argumentative, annoying and blames others.
- *'Wheeler-dealer'*: charming, manipulative, self-centred, impatient, often dishonest.
- *Identity search*: underachievers, self-absorbed, opinionated, determinedly independent.
- *Depressed or sad*: indecisive, listless, apathetic, sleep or eat too much, pessimistic about everything.

Of course, we struggle to believe that these characteristics – *disinclinations* – are immovably embedded in our students' DNA, and we are particularly uncomfortable when students who seem to fit these descriptions are *defined* by such characteristics. If our starting point is that some students are *not* hard-wired to underachieve then giving some thought to Yuichi Shoda's *context principle* is almost certainly a way forward. Shoda maintains that *individual behaviour cannot be explained or predicted apart from a particular situation, and the influence of a situation cannot be specified without reference to the individual experiencing it* (2007). Addressing issues of underachievement, in short, requires an understanding of the individual *and* an understanding of the situation surrounding that individual. It's too easy, and only partially productive, to say that poverty or low levels of family support, or one of those problematic characteristics or collections of symptoms listed above, explain *everything*. It's a combination of factors, and what happens in school is just as much a part of a child's 'culture' as the language they speak at home, peer group pressures, family values – and by that we mean high as well as indifferent expectations – and economic pressures. This list of the realities that indicate and lie behind underachievement can appear overwhelming and we might feel that alleviating or changing any of these factors through the way we organise and deliver learning might seem beyond us as teachers. Similarly, changing the behaviours of individual underachievers might require a good deal more than simply telling them to behave differently – or covering our classroom walls with inspirational posters and expecting that as a result our disengaged students will experience some sort of epiphany which will transform their worldview and their levels of achievement. When we perceive potential in a student, we cannot be satisfied unless we make some effort to find our way through this complex maze of interdependent variables.

We can't talk about underachievement without taking a brief but necessary detour into issues of gender – and how those issues can often collide with the demands of the curriculum. In the UK, when we talk about gender we invariably mean boys, and more particularly those poor white boys who are being left behind, not only by girls but by boys from ethnic minority cultures. It's about culture not biology – just as intelligence is about a lot more than DNA. These boys are highly visible, too often physically confident but verbally limited and less able to control impulses.

Elsewhere, Natalie Rathvon argues that in practice, when faced with the recalcitrant underachiever, teachers and parents tend to opt for one of two approaches: they increase *control* or they give up trying to engage the child (1996). Like Shoda with his context principle, Rathvon suggests an alternative: instead of trying to change the child, try to change the context – by which she means, change the way adult and child interact and communicate and at the same time change or adapt teaching approaches and materials. Rathvon would say that able students become one of those 'types' of underachievers listed above particularly when the work in the classroom is chronically slow and under-challenging, when they feel isolated from their peers, when the dominant culture of the classroom conforms to a negative peer attitude towards learning or when much of what the teacher does shows that they do not really care for the work or for the student. She would argue that poor white boys are more likely than anyone else to be susceptible to these shortfalls in the learning context.

In her 2016 article about boys, Hinsliff concludes:

> Some boys (not to mention girls) are bored witless in school – but it sure beats a lifetime of low-paid, insecure jobs . . . success doesn't usually fall into the laps of those who didn't do the homework. Boys need role models who don't seek to glamorise slacking, winging it or sneering at the smart kids; who make it cool to stretch yourself at school, and can tap into their competitive instincts. But above all they need grown men to champion them not by lashing out at girls, but cheerfully equipping boys to compete.

We should add, as did a letter in response to Gaby Hinsliff's article, that apart from the social and economic context experienced by learners, underachievement is about more than individual students and teachers, it's about the curriculum they are obliged to contend with (Boffy, 2016). It's the context principle writ large – league tables, tests, PISA, the whole lot – and not least the stalemate that occurs when curriculum and learner mean absolutely nothing to each other. Boffy calls what he sees as a one size-fits-all curriculum an *ill-fitting garment* when what is needed if we are to truly motivate young people is *bespoke tailoring*. Other correspondents to the letters page were similarly annoyed by Hinsliff's contention that we ought to *just tell* these boys to *knuckle down* insisting that today's schools *do* value more than the things learned while sitting down (Mitchell, 2016) or included in the data to beat schools with or for countries to use to win the 'top test scores' competition with other countries.

Where did the motivation go and are we to blame?

The bottom line is, as they say, is motivation. When there is a lack of motivation and achievement, where did we, parents and teachers, go wrong? Is it our fault that the motivation went missing? There is a controversial but nevertheless interesting short book called, *The Underachiever's Manifesto* by Ray Bennett (2006) which argues, only half-jokingly, that if we *tug too hard on one thread the whole thing unravels*[1]. This is a version of the Taoist saying: *Fill your bowl to the brim and it will overflow*, or of Picasso's advice that: *You must always work not just within, but below your means. If you can handle three elements, handle only two. In that way, the ones you do handle, you handle with more ease, more mastery, and you create a feeling of strength in reserve* (Jones, 2016). All of which begs the question (and it isn't as daft as it sounds): have we been tugging too hard on too limited or too diverse a range of threads – ones selected and pursued single-mindedly by the curriculum, the school, the teacher and the family? It must be said (quickly) that we are not mentioning Bennett's book to counter those concepts we so admire – like 'desirable difficulty' and 'tension to learn' – or Duckworth's insistence on a need to teach 'grit' – that word which is her interpretation of a phrase often used by successful creative people when asked how they got to where they are today: *If you want to do it, pursue it.*

As we said in the chapter on an agenda for the more able (Chapter 3) motivation is built upon individual needs, it is 'first-person'; once ignited, a 'third person' is added to the mix – the teacher or the examination syllabus – and once these elements have happened the learning becomes, implicitly, *first-person plural*. What students experience and encounter in, or because of, the classroom and the home must become part of themselves. Learning – and achievement – is a collective thing, a co-operative process. If we fail to see learning as this co-operative or as Vygotsky would say, co-constructed activity, then motivation is likely to fade away – if it ever catches on in the first place. Co-construction is about two things: collaboration between teacher, students and peers in order to solve a problem, and at the same time constructing what Vygotsky calls a *joint problem space*. A productive, engaging and supportive climate for learning: *What a child can do today in cooperation, tomorrow he will be able to do on his* own (Vygotsky 1962).

So, we get it wrong when everything our students experience is in the third-person, when the threads are second hand threads and what's worse, when we do not even allow to student to hold those threads unmediated because of that 'anxious literalism' that makes everything we do about reaching the required, and often minimum, grades. Our approach to motivation, in these circumstances, becomes about *extrinsic motivation*: We spoon feed: we practice 'layer-cake teaching' – frequent repetition and rigid adherence to the core curriculum – our teaching is entirely goal-oriented, which means the rewards are offered by teachers and are all in the future. A recent online survey about how American High School students feel about school, found that the most common answer was *bored, tired and stressed* (Lathram, 2016). Lathram quotes the creator of the musical *Hamilton*, Lin Manuel Miranda describing boredom as the 'font of creativity' and a prominent US educator, Nancy Flanagan, urging parents to, *tell your kids to own their own boredom and fix it*. When these are the results of a learner's experience in school, then isn't it because the 'rewards' for learning are not happening in the present, they are a vague promise, not a tangible reality? The opposite of extrinsic motivation is *intrinsic* motivation which is about learning driven by absorption and interest. How we help create this state, comes later.

So, if changing or enhancing commitment is not about pep talks, offering top grades, inspirational posters and frightening students with stories of a bleak future without achievement, what is it about?

Rediscovering motivation: a change of tack?

Having expressed a certain amount of cynicism about inspirational texts we are now going to quote one. It's from *The Sword in the Stone* by T.H. White:

> 'The best thing for being sad,' replied Merlin . . . 'is to learn something. That's the only thing that never fails. You may grow old and trembling in your anatomies, . . . you may miss your only love, you may see the world around you devastated by evil lunatics. . . . There is only one thing for it then – to learn. Learn why the world wags and what wags it. That is the only thing which the mind can never exhaust, never alienate, never be tortured by, never fear or distrust, and never dream of regretting. Learning is the only thing for you. Look what a lot of things there are to learn.'

If nothing else, this reminds us that, *the world is an inexhaustibly diverting, inspiring, fascinating place* (Leslie, 2014) yet as importantly, the 'sadness' that Merlin is addressing in White's story echoes through all of those symptoms and varieties of underachievement listed earlier. Whatever the students think they achieve from not achieving it certainly isn't happiness or fulfilment.

Which brings us to the artist, Andy Warhol and the musician, John Cage. Warhol said, *I like boring things*. He meant that many things just *seem* boring, like a can of baked beans, but that is because we are not giving them our full attention (Wilson 2004). John Cage said: *If something is boring for two minutes, try it for four. If still boring, then eight. Then sixteen. Then thirty-two. Eventually one discovers it is not boring at all* (Popova 2012). Try to experience what James Ward, who writes a blog called 'I like boring things' calls, *the transformative power of attention*. Looking at what Georges Perec (2010) calls, *the infra-ordinary* – the opposite of the *extra-ordinary* and what Warhol and Cage are urging – find ways to make life interesting, try, as Henry James said: *To be one of those people upon whom nothing is lost* (1888). Perhaps this is Duckworth's 'grit' or maybe it's more about finding ways to keep learners curious.

The question we have to ask of teachers and parents at this point is how much do they help or hinder a motivation? We quoted Erik Shonstrom earlier, where he argues that learning, *is inherently dynamic and propulsive, not sedentary and passive* but that *most traditional instruction depends on the latter state and seeks to control the former* (2014). So how do we, perhaps not deliberately, 'control' that natural desire and need to learn; how do we hinder motivation? Four of the ways we mismanage motivation are:

- Through fear: of getting it wrong, of asking questions, of failing, of a chaotic classroom or home, of being mocked. When the 'comfort zone' is somewhere else the child will inevitably be fearful of new experiences, new ideas, new learning.
- By constant disapproval: by saying 'don't' in almost every situation – don't talk, don't shout, don't interrupt, don't leave your seat, don't ask silly questions, don't

get dirty, don't touch – and so on and so on. This is the best way to quash a desire to explore and discover.

- By overdoing the complexity, the unfamiliarity and the uncertainty – taking the notion of 'desirable difficulty' too far with the result that the willingness to explore is squashed.
- By *not* being there: by taking Rousseau too much to heart and not providing a safe, supportive and interested setting in which the child can share the results of their explorations, discoveries and learning.

Which begs the question – if this is what we are doing and if we are, how do we put it right?

1. If you want your child or class not to fail, stop seeing what they do as failure.
   When the results of a child's effort go wrong but they keep trying to find ways to make them go right, that is not failure, it's persistence and resilience. Recent educational thinkers, such as Guy Claxton, argue that resilience is the most valuable quality that we should try to nurture. Learning is often a long job which involves longer-term commitment. If a child keeps getting something wrong over and over again, that's not failure, that's determination.
2. Attention and approval, particularly of effort and conscientiousness, will best reinforce the desire to learn.
   If you see the child's responses are off-piste, redirect, rather than squash them. Sometimes curiosity can seem frivolous or trivial, or misdirected, but it is important that it is recognised. When we brush off what appears to be an irrelevant question, it might be that we are simply not hearing what the child is saying.
3. Quite simply – model curiosity.
   Students should see in us what we want to see in them – an openness to new information and ideas.
4. Educational Psychologist, Daniel Willingham, makes the point that:
   Sometimes I think that we, as teachers are so eager to get to the answers that we do not devote sufficient time to getting the questions right (2009). Questions ignite curiosity, being given answers squashes curiosity. Good questions expose an information gap that allows for thinking, discussion and exploration.
5. To get the process of acquiring new knowledge moving, says Lowenstein, **we** have got to 'prime the pump', with some new and possibly incomplete information (1994). There is a good deal to be said for the belief that achievement and knowledge drives motivation.

In our classrooms, how do we 'prime the pump' on a daily basis?

Never mind the theory, feel the practicalities:

1. Encourage, cultivate, and embrace discussion.
2. Create the curious classroom or home environment bursting with complexities that invite questions.

3. Provide visible and ongoing learning projects – ones without easy answers and then invite the sort of discussion and collaboration on these projects that encourages:

*   'Could be' answers that invite speculation.
*   Learning out loud: externalises thinking, emotions, decision making.
*   Paying attention to challenging but manageable gaps in knowledge.
*   Exploring the notion of 'desirable difficulty' and how an element of struggle stimulates learning and remembering.
*   Opportunities to meet the unexpected, to explore and solve problems; is open to serendipity – the accidental connection, the unintended error. Models the adult's curiosity by how you respond to unforeseen events or ideas in the lesson. (Remember that school inspectors are particular impressed by your capacity to create learning that promotes the unexpected.)
*   Giving time for learners to find answers: '*it's not what adults do to children – it's what the child does for him or herself*' – and considers the importance of peer interaction, that thinking occurs between children as much as it does within children (Engel, 2015). Avoids too much focus on the fasted thinkers; uses 'think–pair–share' to allow for thinking and private discussion time.
*   Asking questions – but does not accept first answers, avoids 'surface slide', presses for justifications and 'second question' to take the discussion further.
*   Not intervening too early when learners are blocked; let them find a solution – and fail if necessary. Talk about strategies to overcome blocks.
*   Being open and honest, admitting when you do not know or find something hard, talk about your own learning – share the struggle.
*   Don't paraphrase – but insist that learners paraphrase each other.
*   Remove the stigma of being wrong. Encourage curiosity into the causes of errors – use them not as an indication of failure, but as an index of what needs to be learned.
*   Try a 'three-before-me' approach when learners encounter difficulties – ask for solutions from three of the peer group before approaching the teacher.

4. Set up 'reporters' on group discussions.
5. Try not being too precise with learning objectives, but rather let them emerge out of the discussion.
6. Use a 'questions for next lesson' board on to which students can post outstanding queries or interest.

*   'Before I read or hear your work, can *you* give me two ways you could have improved it?'

Achievement, motivated teachers and learners. What are we looking for?

The conventional response to individual or group underachievement is to think in terms of intervention strategies. These might involve individual counselling, or comparing approaches with other teachers and with the student's family to establish issues and expectations. In the initial stages, intervention programmes such as these take control away from the child, on the grounds that we create habits in the leaners of being unable to work independently in their own best interest. We are not arguing that such student-centred approaches are inappropriate. They may well prove effective, but only if all those involved, students, teachers, parents, peer-group and counsellors, find effective ways of working together. Like high quality differentiation, such an approach is a big ask for teachers. Of course, we are intensely focused on individual learners, as the long list of strategies listed above would confirm, but we have tended towards a more inclusive vision for the students, the class and the teacher.

It is probably obvious that what we would hope to see, and what underlies much of what we think about the work of teacher, might be summed up in Samuel Beckett's plea for persistence: *No matter. Try again. Fail again. Fail better* (1969) – coupled with Andre Gide's urge for us to remain open to new ideas: *one does not discover new lands without consenting to lose sight of the shore for a very long time* (1973); and finally, so that we do not forget just how surprising our students can be, Ben Marcus', *if we are not sometimes baffled and amazed and undone by the world around us, rendered speechless and stunned, perhaps we are not paying close enough attention* (2015). Warhol again – and Cage and Henry James.

An achieving classroom, which happens when we are *paying close enough attention*, should look like this:

- Students and the teacher have high expectations demonstrated by a mutual enthusiasm for learning. All are responsive to new insights, and all are included in the lesson's conversations. Meta-cognitive (learning to learn) strategies, such as summarising, questioning, clarifying and predicting, are taught as well as practised.
- There is an intense level of engagement and shared responsibility. Students self-regulate, are comfortable with peer-assisted learning and two-way questioning; learning is active, not passive. Feedback, similarly, is two-way – from as well as to the students – and is explicitly aimed at achieving subject mastery. Students are well on the way to becoming independent in thought and action.
- Activities go well beyond the functional; are designed to stretch, encourage unpredicted responses and go well beyond the requirements of the course or the final examination.
- Learning is interpersonal: the struggle is shared, difference and individuality is valued, and enjoyment is palpable.

Last words

Early on in this chapter we made passing reference to Lynsey Hanley's 2007 book, *Estates: An Intimate History* and used her phrase, *a wall in the head* to describe the sort of resistance to learning we sometimes meet in our classrooms. Hanley's argument is that the monotony of the built environment, as seen in many public housing projects, actually creates and reproduces this *wall in the head*. They induce a state of mind which builds *invisible barriers* to knowledge, self-improvement and social mobility. She says that they *sap the spirit, suck out hope and ambition, and draw in apathy and nihilism*.

These are powerful words and we do not for a minute suggest that all of the schools in such places have an identical impact – and yet we do recognise her description as relevant to what may have been, if only for brief periods, our own classroom experiences. What we are warning against is a situation in any school, serving whatever population and place, where those invisible barriers created by underachievement and defeated motivation are allowed to exist – persist even – and as a result *suck out hope and ambition*. Everything we have written in this book is about how we need to work against the atrophying of learning in our classroom, which can so easily be the result of the 'anxious literalism' brought about through second-guessing what examination syllabi and government diktats want us to do, rather than what students tell us they need. If we meet those *walls in the head* in our classrooms we have to be sure that we didn't build or reinforce them, and more than that, we have done everything in our power to break them down.

Note

1   This phrase comes from a 2012 *Guardian* article about Bennett's book by Oliver Burkeman: 'This column will change your life.'

References

Beckett, S.: 'Samuel Beckett Talks About Beckett' interview with John Gruen; *Vogue*, December 1969.

Bennett, R.: *The Underachiever's Manifesto: The Guide to Accomplishing Little and Feeling Great*; San Francisco, CA: Chronicle Books 2006.

Boffy, R.: Letter; *The Guardian* 21.11.16.

Burkeman, O.: 'This column will change your life;' *The Guardian* 2012.

Engel, S.: *The Hungry Mind*; Cambridge, MA: Harvard 2015.

Gide, A.: *The Counterfeiters*; New York: Vintage 1973.

Goethe, Johann: Wilhelm Meister's Apprenticeship; A Novel. TheClassics.us (2013).

Hanley, Lynsey: *Estates: An Intimate History*; London: Granta 2007.

Hinsliff, G.: 'Our Boys need to be rescued, and it's take a new kind of role model'; *The Guardian* 18.11.2016.

James, H.: 'The Art of Fiction'; *Longman's Magazine* 1888.

Jones, O.: 'In praise of underachievement'; BigThink.com 2016. Available at: http://bigthink.com/ ideafeed/in-praise-of-underachievement.

Karaduman, G.B.: 'Underachievement in Gifted Students': *International Journal on New Trends in Education and Their Implications*; October 2013.

Lathram, B.: *Ideas for Combating Boredom in School*; 2016. Available at: www.gettingsmart.com/2016/07/9 -ideas-for-combatting-boredom-in-school-and-why-being-bored-may-not-be-all-bad/.

Leslie, I.: *Curious: The desire to know and why your future depends on it*; London: Quercus 2014.

Lowenstein, G.: 'The Psychology of Curiosity'; *Psychological Bulletin* 1994.

Mandel, H.P. and Marcus, S.I.: *The Psychology of Underachievement: differential diagnosis and differential treatment*; Hoboken, NJ: Wiley 1988.

Marcus, B.: *New American Stories*; London: Granta 2015.

Mitchell, P.: Letter; *The Guardian* 21.11.16.

Perec, G.: *An attempt at exhausting a place in Paris*; Adelaide: Wakefield Press 2010.

Popova, M.: 'Where the heart beats: John Cage'; 2012. Available at www.brainpickings.org/2012/07/ 05/where-the-heart-beats-john-cage-kay-larson.

Rathvon, N.: *The Unmotivated Child*; London: Simon and Schuster 1996.

Reis, S.M. and McCoach, D.B.: 'The Underachievement of Gifted Students: What We Know and Where Do We Go?' *Gifted Child Quarterly* 2000.

Roach, J.: *Austin Powers: The Spy Who Shagged Me*; 1999.

Shoda, Y.: *The Person in Context: Building a Science of the Individual*; New York: Guilford Press 2007.

Shonstrom, E.: *Education Week* 2014.

Ward, J. iamjamesward.com

White, T.H.: *The Sword in the Stone*; New York: Collins Modern Classics 2008.

Willingham, D.: *Why Don't Students Like School?*; San Francisco, CA: Jossey-Bass 2009.

Wilson, W.: 'Prince of Boredom: The Repetitions and Passivities of Andy Warhol' 2004. Available at www.warholstars.org/prince-boredom-warhol-william-wilson.html.

Chapter 12

The journey to university

The long haul?

One of the most significant reasons for the renewed focus on the more able in the UK is that national data reveals that hundreds of schools fail to produce any students suitable for elite universities. Almost a quarter of England's sixth forms and colleges had no pupils with the top A-level grades sought by leading institutions. Why are 300+ schools effectively written off – or, more specifically the students they teach, who will never have the chance of attending a top university? Even if it is conceded that many students may not want to go there, or don't feel it is for them, there will be hundreds who would perhaps have liked the opportunity at least. This problem is not a UK one alone.

A tiny number of independent schools send more youngsters to Oxbridge than thousands of state secondary schools. Independent school students were more than twice as likely as students in comprehensive schools or academies to be accepted into one of the 30 most highly selective universities. One hundred schools, comprising 87 independent schools and 13 grammar schools (just 3% of schools with sixth forms and sixth form colleges in the United Kingdom), accounted for over a tenth (11.2%) of admissions to highly selective universities during the three-year period (Koppel, 2014).

The recent Ofsted reports on More Able in 2013 and 2015 also look at how these students make decisions about university applications and what support they need to be successful. They make the entirely incontrovertible point that schools must work with families more closely, particularly the families of first-generation university applicants and those eligible for free school meals, to overcome any cultural and financial obstacles to university application. The support and guidance provided to students when they were thinking about, and applying for, university varied in quality, accuracy and depth in the schools that Ofsted surveyed, with a lack of up-to-date, in-school intelligence about applications. Although most of the schools considered themselves to be providing good support and guidance, around half of them accepted any university as an option and did not have aspirations that their students should aim to apply to leading universities.

The study Studies have also indicated that the difference in the admission rates to highly selective universities could not be attributed solely to the schools' average A-level or equivalent results. Fifty-eight per cent of higher education applicants from the 30 best comprehensive schools (with average scores for students exceeding three A grades at A level) were accepted into the 30 most highly selective universities. This compared with 87.1% of applicants from the 30 best independent schools and 74.1% from the 30 best grammar schools (Ofsted 2010 and 2013). The key here is to look at the longer-term issues schools face. It is all too common to hear schools wondering aloud, for instance, why none of their most able students ever get into top universities. When they are gently steered towards looking more closely at their UCAS preparations, their interviewing schedules, the odd choices that their students might be making at KS4, and the passivity and quietness of their students, they often realise that the data has not been illustrating a long-term discrimination against their school, but rather their own long-term failure to investigate what their data has been telling them about their own practices. Schools' expertise in and knowledge about how to apply to the most prestigious universities were not always current and relevant. Insufficient support and guidance were provided to those most able students whose family members had not attended university. Other than time, what might the reasons be for this lack of engagement with leading universities?

Do you think our quiet quads can contain your passion?

In the first scene of Tamsin Oglesby's play, *Future Conditional*[1], the seventeen-year-old Alia is being interviewed for a place to read English at an Oxford College. When asked why she wants to come to University she says, *I would like to help mend the cracks in the landscape*. Alia wants to become a teacher, because, *where I come from girls have no education*, and, *things must change*. Learning, she says, has taught her *that there can be more reality on the page than on the ground* and, thanks to an inspiring English teacher, literature has saved her life. More precisely, it has saved her **inner life**. The poet and dramatist Tony Harrison's passion for learning was also ignited by his family and social background: *I was hoping to express things my parents and uncles had never been able to express* (2017). He grew up alongside an uncle who was dumb and another who stammered and so was aware on an almost daily basis of the *wound of inarticulacy*. Like Alia in the play, Harrison's *great hunger* was satisfied *by the greatest food*; in his case, it was Greek literature and drama – which began in school and developed at Cambridge University. Quoting Arthur Scargill's[2] reference to his father: *My father reads the dictionary every day. He says your life depends on your power to master words*, Harrison insists that for him too, mastering words has been *the* important struggle.

Tamsin Oglesby and Tony Harrison would say that it is the injustice they see in the world around them – the *wound of inarticulacy* and the denial of a decent education for girls across the world – that, to paraphrase Brecht's phrase, is what drives them to sit at their desks, learn and write. In our eyes, the answer to the question about why we should try to convince students that a place at university is worth pursuing is partly, if not wholly, answered by this *passion* to change the world, or at least to experience *the greatest food* that might be found in the reality of the academic 'world of the page' – and what that experience might offer to our understanding of our inner selves and of the world around us. The learning and the experience on offer at university is an important way for individuals to be challenged by the latest ideas. They invite students into the world of academic pursuit, of knowledge, research, theories and first-hand experience, but more than that, they are about the networking of all those ideas and thoughts – internationally as well as locally.

Hardly silent activities suited best to the *quiet quads* of learning. This phrase is from the Oglesby play, used by a tutor who is puzzled that a girl with Alia's background (an unaccompanied migrant supported by a series of foster families) should want to go to a university of inward-looking academics. Given the chance he would probably add that she should look at a course where learning was given a 'real life' rather than an academic context – even that she should consider distance learning alongside work experience in a setting where she could earn and learn at the same time. An internship, perhaps, rather than an academic course.

Clive James' 1980 article in *The Listener* mentions that Shakespeare's Hamlet and Horatio find very different things at their university in Wittenberg: two close and loyal friends who do not see the benefits of university in the same way. James thinks that Horatio's horizon is bounded by what he describes as Wittenberg's *port and walnuts and the relative safety of academic intrigue*. Like many of the distinctly able students we teach, the *quiet quads* of university would suit Horatio down to the ground. He would see them not just as a haven for engrossing study but also as an investment in his future, an expansion of his CV, as professional training in transferable skills, a foothold in the job market and access to the university's networks of influence – and most of all perhaps, as a promise of secure financial prospects and a quiet life in the world to come. Hamlet, on the other hand, has a restless imagination. He needs to question what everyone else seems to accept is the truth; he would see the *quiet quads* as a battleground rather than a refuge. He would know exactly what Tony Harrison and Tamsin Oglesby are talking about – he too wants to fix *the cracks in the landscape* and heal the *wound of inarticulacy* – once he can pin down exactly what those 'cracks' and 'wounds' are. Clearly, in real life those students who use the university experience to find ways to question and find ways to change the world are almost certainly more likely make a better fist of it than Hamlet manages. Hamlet's 'default setting' is procrastination: of course, he questions his inability to act but that doesn't seem to help – until it is too late. If circumstances had allowed, Hamlet's university at Wittenberg would have been a much safer bet that the rain-soaked battlements of Elsinore. Academic intrigue beats real world intrigue any day.

Which is all a long-winded way of saying that the first step on the path to university is for a student to work out exactly why they want to go there in the first place. It might be out of a passion for a subject, a chance to meet like-minded people, a useful CV item or even a chance of a rewarding career in the future but it does need thinking through – not least as that question will need an answer, either in the personal statement or in an interview. Why take on all that debt? Shakespeare didn't go to university, neither did Albert Einstein, nor the playwrights Osbourne, Pinter and Stoppard; the publisher Penguin and the accountancy firm Ernst and Young no longer require candidates to have a university degree. The common view that many employers will not consider seriously people without a degree seems to be less prevalent, and of course, more individuals are returning to study later in life when they are really motivated and can afford the fees.

Which university?

The quick answer might be that Hamlet, as Prince of Denmark, probably had someone to do his choosing for him – his father, the Old Hamlet, perhaps? Had he enjoyed more independence he would, like most students do today, have sent off to the UK for *The Complete University Guide* and made up his own mind. His interest may have been aroused by the knowledge that Wittenberg was a Lutheran University, a place associated with political dissent and he certainly would have liked the Protestant idea of individual responsibility. His own country Denmark would have probably hoped he would attend a Catholic university, so in choosing Wittenberg, he was perhaps asserting his independence and individuality.

If, as Coleridge said: *It is **we** who are Hamlet* (1992) – what questions about which university might we have in common? Do we want to stay close to home or get as far away as possible? City, small town, or semi-rural? Full-time or part-time? Which course? De we have a career in mind and is there a course which is a necessary qualification for that job? Have we looked at the university's website and planned an open day visit?

After these first questions, there is much more to discover. Using data from the Higher Education Statistics Agency (HESA), the Higher Education Funding Council for England (HEFCE), the Scottish Higher Education Funding Council (SHEFC) and the Higher Education Funding Council for Wales (HEFCW), *The Complete University Guide* provides potential students with a plethora of data and information about what each university offers and how it performs. There is detail on entry standards; student-staff ratios; spending on academic services and facilities; records for good honours degrees, graduate prospects, completion rates and international enrolments. Added to this there are scores to measure student satisfaction, research quality and research intensity. Then there are other sources which might feed further a student's need to know and decide: *The Guardian* newspaper, for instance, publishes university league tables in the Spring of each year. It uses the National Student Survey (NSS), which takes views from 220,000 final year students and uses a two-year average of responses in their final tables. It measures teaching quality, the effectiveness of assessment and feedback, and overall student satisfaction. The tables also include value-added scores based on students' progress taking the qualifications they had at the start of the course, and comparing them with the qualifications achieved on completion of their degree. Alternatively, there is a website called Unistats which gives a comprehensive guide to courses of study – a Key Information Set (KIS) designed to help students make informed choices about which course at which university. And if they are still not sure, there's The Stamford Test for students who don't know what their passions are – yet.

Of course, having read through all this, we would hope that Hamlet did not discover that he had made some wrong choices with his A level course – as 41% of students reported they had in a 2016 TES survey. Horatio was almost certainly prepared and cautious: he would have gone for a university subject with which he was familiar. Hamlet would have been more adventurous; he would have wanted to feel passionate about the course of study, he would want his imagination to be fired and remain in flames for the next three years.

Why would a university want you?

When a student writes that crucial 4000-character **personal statement** they are expected to include a clear indication of the academic and the cultural capital (see Glossary) that they would be bringing to and taking from that university. In other words, how diverse a collection of knowledge would they bring, and how eager are they to share the expertise being offered by the university? This is about more than saying why they want *that* university, it's about why they want *that subject*, what has drawn them to it, what they could add to it. Why they and their chosen subject were clearly made for each other. In the personal statement, and later in interview should the opportunity arise, the applicant needs a way to show – in a controlled and careful way – something resembling Tamsin Oglesby's and Tony Harrison's passion and sense of mission. At the same time, university tutors would expect evidence of that passion in the ways that the student had pursued that subject beyond school and the requirements of an examination syllabus. Both Alia, the character from the play, and the dramatist who created her, seem to be driven more than anything by the cultural importance of their subject and its potential to change, or at least make a solid contribution, to the world. They seem determined to challenge a world where whole populations are deprived of a voice because of class, race, gender, wealth or politics. If either Tamsin Oglesby or Tony Harrison were asked, as is a student in the personal statement, to say why they seem to favour the cultural over the academic importance of university, they would no doubt cite their track record of performed plays, and how what they write involves a conscious interplay between actors and audience, and an engagement with current political issues.

Whichever sort of student individuals believe themselves to be, they are going to have to *prove* their passion for the subject applied for. They are going to have to articulate that passion and at the same time, offer examples of how they have put that passion into practice in their own lives. The conventional way to illustrate this with relevant extracurricular activities. The character in Oglesby's play doesn't have any extracurricular activities to prove her commitment; as one of the tutors she meets at the university interview points out, she has had no family who would take her camping, or pay for her to learn to play an instrument or go skiing. What she does have, however, is a startling ability to unravel, understand and use unconventional arguments to deconstruct a piece of writing she has been given to talk about. Nevertheless, the personal statement is a balance: academic passion together with thought-through encounters with the wider context of the subject on the student's application form. In short, show a unique understanding of the subject and its potential.

The interview

In a recent survey of independent school students who had secured a place at either Oxford or Cambridge, they were asked what they believed had been key to their success (LGT, 2016). They gave a series of quite distinct answers:

1. Their school gave them a list of books that, as one student said, *let me into the subject.* Knowing about the subject means more than knowing the examination syllabus. Answering questions about why the student was drawn to that subject might well be found in the extended reading they have undertaken. Why *this* subject is very often the first question an interviewer asks and in giving the answer there is opportunity to show commitment and passion. Reading widely around a subject is not solely about books: there are websites, newspaper features, journal and magazines. Oxford University, among others, also has a website listing, subject by subject, recommended reading.[3]

2. The school students talked about preparing for an Oxbridge interview by stepping back from the detail of what they know already and considering *the bigger questions* that a discipline addresses. This means, essentially, being able to show how that subject might contribute to an understanding of society, its development and view of itself. The question itself might encourage a broad rather than detailed aspects of the subject. How political is literature? Why do you think dementia is more common in developed countries? Are criminals born or made? Should bankers earn a large salary? Going beyond the syllabus is, for these students who responded to the survey,

not only about finding and engaging critically with the bigger ideas inherent in their subject, but also in thinking about how their subject relates to other disciplines.

3. The school helped these students with their preparation by encouraging interview practice and by inviting visitors to the school who were experts in their field. The visitors often prompted something of a shift in perspective. Seeing the subject in a fresh and newly relevant way together with the practice taught them to *roll with the punches* – talk about subject related issues in conversation rather than in quiz show mode. University interviews are about uncovering a student's *thinking* processes, whether they can unpick a question logically, creatively and with a degree of original thinking, rather than simply about what they know already.

Interviews are not so much about proven ability, but rather they are about potential, hence the need to treat them as conversations – or even as tutorials where the opinions the student gives are only a part of the process. How they listen, what they ask, how they challenge and disagree, how they argue a point, how they evaluate existing knowledge and demonstrate their passion and intense interest in what they hope to study are all part of the interview process. The tutor on the other side of the room wants to know not so much what a student's mind contains in terms of 'cultural capital' but what a student's mind has the potential to achieve in terms of thinking and creating. Of course, Pierre Bourdieu's notion of *cultural capital* – that breadth of subject knowledge which can give any conversation shared reference points – helps the conversation tick along.

All of this is not just a checklist for students as they prepare themselves for an interview, it's a checklist for subject teachers as they support the process. Even just pointing students towards books and reading beyond the syllabus is an obvious way to encourage, inviting subject experts into school is another, but perhaps the two most important drivers towards what the student hopes to achieve are:

•   Providing a classroom experience built on discussion, an interplay of questions and the exchange of ideas.
•   An openness to serendipity – to accidental discoveries, connections and unexpected insights.

But for a more targeted and planned approach, some of the guidance below may prove to be useful.

What works well in ensuring high rates of progression to universities?

Immediate engagement with students, and ideally their parents/carers, about the next steps in their educational career beyond school that starts at the transition from primary to secondary. Training for staff on academic subject choices and the content and requirements of degree courses to help them to provide support and guidance for students around the decision-making process. This needs to be followed by a planned programme for raising students' awareness of university education, also delivered early and regularly promoted, followed by sessions on applying to UCAS, completing personal statements, and understanding the financial implications and benefits of attending university. Students should be encouraged to visit a range of universities to broaden their horizons and aspirations and to speak to ex-students currently attending university.

There also needs to be a strong focus from the earliest possible age on the personal and academic development of more able students with a clear emphasis on gaining admission to a top university. This should help students to develop systematically the skills and knowledge they require to make informed choices as well as confidence, independence, and enthusiasm for learning. When they get closer to application, a focus on their wider reading will pay dividends.

So, what do successful applicants for top universities do?

Successful candidates for elite universities delve a little further into their subject areas through independent reading, not because they have to, but because they have a genuine love for their subject. By reading around their subject they not only demonstrate their commitment, they are also immersing themselves in the essence of the discipline. As a direct result, they have more interesting things to say in their personal statement, as well as at interview. It gives them the opportunity to think about the harder questions and to tackle some of the more interesting issues that they will face on their course. It allows them to use real detail from their independent reading to structure arguments and to understand what the course might entail and why it might be a good fit for them. The admissions tutors will have dedicated their lives to their subject, and they will not be convinced by a student trying to 'wing it'. Unless it is clear that the student shares their enthusiasm for the course disciplines they will soon see through the lack of commitment and desire.

A brief selection of books to help to explore your subject:

*   **Architecture**
    Towards a New Architecture by Le Corbusier
    The Timeless Way of Building by Christopher Alexander
*   **Anthropology**
    The Selfish Gene by Richard Dawkins
    The Origin of Species by Charles Darwin
*   **Chemistry**
    Foundations of Organic Chemistry by Michael Hornby and Josephine Peach
    The Periodic Table by Eric R. Scerri
*   **Classics**
    The Iliad by Homer
    Classics: A Short Introduction by Mary Beard and John Henderson
*   **Computer Science**
    An Introduction of Algorithms by Thomas Cormen
    The Emperor's New Mind by Roger Penrose
*   **Economics**
    The Ascent of Money by Niall Ferguson
    Too Big To Fail by Andrew Ross Sorkin

- **Education**
    Fifty Modern Thinkers On Education edited by Joy Palmer
    How Children Think and Learn by David Wood
- **English**
    The Great Tradition by F.R. Leavis
    Literary Theory by Terry Eagleton
- **Engineering Science**
    Cat's Paws and Catapults by Steven Vogel
    Invention by Design by Henry Petroski
- **Geography**
    Human Geography Edited by John Agnew
    The Geographical Tradition by David Livingstone
- **History**
    A Little History of the World by E.H. Gombrich
    What is History? by E.H. Carr
- **History of Art**
    Studies in Iconology by Erwin Panofsky
    Ways of Seeing by John Berger
- **Law**
    Learning the Law by Glanville Williams
    Eve Was Framed by Helena Kennedy
- **Linguistics**
    The Language Instinct by Steven Pinker
    Through the Language Glass: Why the World Looks Different in Other Languages by Guy Deutscher
- **Mathematics**
    The Mathematical Tourist by Ivars Peterson
    Alice in Numberland by J. Baylis and R. Haggerty
- **Medicine**
    The Man Who Mistook His Wife For A Hat by Oliver Sacks
    The Rise and Fall of Modern Medicine by James Le Fanu
- **Music**
    Nineteenth-century Music by Karl Dahlhaus
    The Norton Anthology of Western Music by Peter Burkholder and Claude Palisca
- **Natural Sciences-Biology**
    The Greatest Show on Earth: The Evidence for Evolution by Richard Dawkins
    How Animals Work by Knut Schmidt Nielson
- **Natural Sciences-Physics**
    Warped Passages: Unravelling the Universe's Hidden Dimensions by Lisa Randall
    A Brief History of Time by Stephen Hawking and Leonard Mlodinow
- **Philosophy**
    What Does It All Mean? by Thomas Nagel
    Science and Wonders by Russell Stannard
- **PPE**
    Anarchy, State and Utopia by Robert Nozick
    Why Humans Have Cultures by Michael Carrithers

- **Theology**
  The Puzzle of Evil and the Puzzle of God by Peter Vardy
  The Early Church by Henry Chadwick

Notes

1   See also the chapter: 'Disturbing the peace', in the companion book: *Redefining English*.
2   Arthur Scargill, leader of the miners' union during the long strike in 1982/3; from the same year in an interview in the *Sunday Times*.
3   www.ox.ac.uk/admissions/undergraduate/courses/suggested-reading-and-resources%20.

References

'A third of university applicants regret A-level choices, survey finds'; *Times Educational Supplement* April 2016.

Coleridge, S.T.: 'Lecture notes'; *The Romantics on Shakespeare*, London: Penguin 1992.

The Complete University Guide; www.thecompleteuniversityguide.co.uk/.

Harrison, T.: *The Inky Digit of Defiance*; London: Faber and Faber 2017.

James, C.: 'Hamlet in Perspective' *The Listener*; Reprinted in *Cultural Cohesion; The essential essays*: New York: Norton 2003.

Koppel, G.: 'Why is Oxbridge taking fewer state school students?'; *The Guardian* 2014.

Ofsted: *Moving through the system – information, advice and guidance (080273)* Ofsted 2010.

Ofsted: *The Most Able Students: Are They Doing as Well as they Should in our Non-Selective Secondary Schools?* Ofsted 2013 and 2015.

Oglesby, T.: *Future Conditional*; London: Oberon Books 2015.

The Stamford Test: www.ucas.com.

Unistats: www.unistats.direct.gov.uk.

Chapter 13

21 ways to shape a whole school culture

Happy landings?

How can we help our most able students from all backgrounds and starting points achieve academic excellence?

1. Focus on longer term narrative arcs

How do we encourage students to plan for learning?

For every unit or topic, we need to approach long- and shorter-term planning with clear ideas about how we want students to develop a genuine understanding of content and how that fits in with how they see our subject area. Sometimes this will be through single, episodic lessons; at other times this needs to be developed across a series of lessons that might take a number of weeks. We need to ensure that our students don't see learning as a lesson by lesson series of easily obtainable learning objectives, but rather see the wider long-term arc across a series of lessons or even across a term or year. Particularly for our more able students, a longer narrative arc means teachers have an increased opportunity to think deeply about the pace of teaching and learning; from the outset of the school year, and in every lesson (and beyond-lesson work), setting a pace that genuinely challenges students and moves their learning on rapidly by capitalising on every possible opportunity for widening their understanding. It also means the chance to think about pace of recall, and how we can ensure that our students are able to secure and consolidate their understanding.

2. Model academic language

How do we establish clear expectations regarding precision in the use of high level subject-specific language?

We don't have to spell the power of language out in mini-lectures or inspirational posters on the wall, we simply have to model it through high level quality immersion in the subject-specific language we use, in our daily teaching. The way that we demonstrate and encourage language use – both in and out of lessons – is key. By our own appropriate use of academic and subject-specific language, we can encourage students to do the same. Make academic and subject-specific language the norm by modelling precise language use all the time, and by pointing out that excellence is a habit, and that we become what we consistently do. Try to get your students accustomed to using language well and spelling accurately, with good punctuation at all times. Lower level academic language skills often hold back high-ability students and we can undermine the significance and point of high level subject-specific language by dumbing down our own language in class, using simplified synonyms. When we are clear in our expectations regarding the accuracy and precision of the technical language we use, we are making it clearer that precision is expected and that it is crucial to feed a higher level of thought and debate.

3. Talk about what supports positive self-concept

How do we ensure students see work and achievement as necessary for self-esteem, not vice versa?

Students need to realise that the effect of achievement on self-concept is stronger than the effect of self-concept on achievement. They must believe that the surest path to positive self-esteem is to succeed at something that they originally perceived would be difficult. We must teach students that grappling with challenges is more important than any amount of easy success, but this becomes a complicated and messy message if we only really reward their successes. Students need to learn how to do hard stuff, to start to feel good about themselves as scholars, and there is a danger that every time we 'steal their struggle' we also take away a chance for them to build confidence (Rimm, 1986). They must learn to do hard things to feel good about themselves and we short circuit the opportunity for them to build self-confidence by accepting their second best. The best way to help students feel that they are succeeding is to help them to actually achieve on their own, but in addition our day to day interactions with them can help to smooth the way for this process. Talk about your own (hopefully) less than perfect learning journey to expertise, to let them know that you, too, needed to go through barriers and that your current confidence has come from an original position of doubt and uncertainty. They see themselves as apprentices and the role of the master in this circumstance is to expose their ignorance to them, so that they understand that they need to keep going to address it.

4. Establish distinct learning and exam preparation phases

How do we separate 'feeding' from 'weighing' the pig?

One of the biggest concerns in many schools is that due to a fixation on national league tables, too much time is spent working out what students know by testing them continually, rather than teaching them what they need to understand to achieve top grades in the first place. Many schools have begun to clearly separate the learning and testing phases, interleaving them as needed. In the learning phase, efforts should be focused solely on developing students' subject knowledge and understanding by nurturing their intellectual curiosity through opportunities for discursive and exploratory learning and high-level problem-solving and risk-taking. Once they have achieved a level of motivation and knowledge then testing becomes useful, as it brings to mind information they don't know, which causes learning to take place. By practising answers students are required to bring to mind information, as well as practising skills such as essay writing, which serve to strengthen memory and learning. Once students have read through how you have marked their work, they should aim to re-draft part or all of it. This will let them know what they are being tested on and what the exam board regard as top grade answers, even if these are below the standards of understanding that they have currently achieved.

5. Consolidate and accredit previous learning

How do we establish what our students already know?

Unless we start from where our students already are, we run the risk of boring them senseless by repetition of already mastered knowledge and concepts. This level of boredom has been highlighted by a great number of schools who have conducted interviews with their most able students, as well as being highlighted by our surveys too. On the other hand, students' poor prior knowledge, together with lack of rigour and knowledge in some GCSE courses, combine to form a weak foundation for progression to A-level learning. Quickly mapping what a class already knows, by using simple techniques such as 'most difficult first', helps to highlight where the pinch points might be regarding any new learning we are embarking upon. Correcting the misconceptions, confusions and misunderstandings from previous learning is critical and helps to provide a solid foundation for future progression. By anticipating and correcting likely student misconceptions, interrogating and challenging their responses, we let them know that previous students have embarked on similar journeys and that we are aware of the inevitable challenges and mistakes that are likely to occur.

6. Clarify what targets are meant to achieve

What do appropriate levels of progress look like for the learner, and how do we transmit that awareness?

We need to be very careful about the setting of target grades, to ensure that they become markers of potential not barriers to progress. The anticipated impact is to highlight a commitment to achievement and to clarify what we expect from our students in the medium term. But many teachers in our surveys are now wondering whether the 'overuse' of target grades may let the achievement of target grades prematurely put a ceiling on learning potential. Peer group influence needs to be highlighted and deconstructed to clearly assert to our students what is required to achieve the top grades and to give them a road map of how to get there. It is essential to explore national versus local standards, as students often believe that what happens in their classroom is an indicator of what the national standards require. As a result, there is a huge danger of limited self-fulfilling prophesies, as students rarely seek acknowledgement beyond their school. They may have little idea therefore of what excellence looks like outside of their limited outlook and experience. The shock often hits them at external examination time or when they first encounter other highly able students at University from very different learning environments.

7. Establish the relevance of your subject

How do we ensure that students understand what our subject is there to do in the world?

We often make a classic hindsight bias assumption when we believe that it will be obvious to our students why they are putting in all this effort for our classes. We need to explain what function our subject performs and what delights it contains for future study, as this is often not clear to our students. By focusing on explaining what our subject gives to the world and what it is there to explain or offer we allow learners greater autonomy and choice. Students need to have these explicitly explained so that they can make the emotional leap necessary to engage fully with what and why we are teaching them. In hundreds of school surveys we've conducted, able students regularly comment that they want to know why things are being studied, what they mean and where they are going next. This allows them a greater sense of progression and an insight 'behind the curtain' of our teaching intentions. In turn this promotes a greater independence and maturity in their responses and engagements.

8. Teach to the top and go 'off-piste'

How do we make explicit what skills and behaviours are required of our learners to achieve beyond the top grades?

If we see able learners as being experts in development, we have to come clean about the fact that becoming an expert is about challenge and struggle within our subject area. It is important to teach outside of the exam requirements and explore the core of your subject. By setting higher levels of challenge and stretch in the tasks we set, in the questions we ask, in the expectations we have of how much our students will cover in and beyond our lessons, we can change their perception of what is possible for them to achieve. We need to teach through deliberately and explicitly demanding tasks and utilise real world problems. We need to explore what features of our subject allow students to properly investigate and research and thereby set up issues and problems that experts in our subject face and deal with. It is very powerful to trial research questions and new technologies, if appropriate, as often as possible and give the students the role of expert in co-development.

9. Define appropriate levels of progress

What does it look like for the learner, and how do we transmit that awareness?

How do we ensure we as teachers know what we're aiming for? How do we let students know what the indicators of excellence are if we don't explicitly point them out to them, and call it whenever they fall short? It is essential to explore national versus local standards as students often believe that what happens in their school is an indicator of what the national standards require. They don't have the opportunities that we teachers have of seeing what happens in other schools, nor do they have a clear understanding of the wider school system and the influences that may bring on results. Peer group influence needs to be highlighted and deconstructed to clearly assert to students what is required to achieve the top grades and to give them a road map of how to get there.

10. Don't reward 'second best' student endeavours

How do we enable students to properly commit to excellence?

Our students need an understanding of what the ethic of excellence looks like with its 'manifesto for craftsmanship' in schools. Across a school there needs to be a consistency that insists that if a piece of work isn't 'perfect', (as good as it can possibly be from that student) it isn't really finished. We need to also commit to training all of our students on how to offer fair and honest feedback to one another. We also ought to demonstrate that any feedback is more useful and effective if questions are used to highlight where work needs to be improved, rather than bald statements that run the risk of simply provoking a negative impact. If students learn to depersonalise any commentary and to add the phrase 'so that . . .' onto any suggestions (in order to explain why the change needs to happen and to make explicit how the work will benefit) then the likelihood of acceptance by the recipient is greatly improved. Students must then get used to formally redrafting their own work, preferably after extensive and regular peer reviews and then more public critique sessions across a class.

11. Change the pace

How do we help students to understand the correct sequencing of events, questions and resources?

Teachers need to set a pace that genuinely challenges the most able students and moves their learning on. Boredom is an all too frequent feeling for the most able students that we teach, based on constantly being asked to revisit concepts already mastered. But teachers also need to be able to recognise when the pace should vary. There is a very real danger that some teachers see pace as synonymous with speed of response or completion rather than more subtle rearrangements and resequencing of tasks. High-ability students have told us they need pockets of time to consolidate and check their understanding – and that they need teachers to check that this is happening. What students do outside the classroom in terms of preparation and homework impacts strongly on progress in class, and school students understand this well. This becomes clearer when we as teachers insist on our own commitment to reading and their commitment to completing set work, driven by their passion for learning and our high expectations.

12. Investigate a variety of narratives

What is the currently successful story behind our subject and why?

In order for our students to have a clearer understanding of our subject, it is important to explore how it has developed over time and why changes happened when they did. All subjects change over time in terms of their focus, the ways they are regarded and the ways they sees themselves. This enables us to introduce to our students the early thinkers and experts whose inferred versions of reality were the currency before the current reigning narrative they know took over. It is vital to locate and explain the texts that have helped to shape our subject and show how they are part of its 'back story.' This raises the issue of where our subject may be going and what still remains to be discovered in the future. This in turn establishes why our students may want to further their studies in our subject area if they choose to investigate it further at University.

13. Normalise extended responses

How do we encourage our students to develop their own chewing muscles?

Teachers often complain of compliance and lack of engagement, with students offering only undeveloped and safe responses to questions. It is important to ensure students are routinely expected to give extended, reasoned answers and are at least given the opportunity to have to defend their viewpoint against rigorous criticism. In order to achieve this, we must take the safety stabilisers off by counteracting the tendency of students to want everything spoon-fed and bite-sized. When students review a topic, passive techniques such as simply reading and highlighting texts have been found to be quite ineffective. We should ensure that students extend their understanding by transforming information into different formats. The whole point of learners seeing themselves as potential developing experts is that they need to grasp the essentials of a subject but also to understand its greater complexities in order to feel how difficult and potentially frustrating becoming a subject scholar can be.

14. Give feedback on best work only

Why are we wasting so much of our time being proofreaders for our students?

Students will learn nothing from any of our detailed commentary on their work unless it is at the very top end of what they can do. If it isn't their best work handed in, then they themselves, with a little thought, can easily make the required changes. Giving students that sense of ownership and responsibility for the development of their work also engages them in the process of improvement. They really need us only when they are in the gap – or liminal space – between knowing and not knowing something. We need to give students the time and encouragement to remain in liminal space for as long as is necessary, as this is precisely where they are more likely to make cognitive changes and master troubling new concepts, rather than simply mimicking what they think we want them to say.

15. Ensure feedback becomes specific directed work for the recipient

Why do we tend to believe that our commitment to marking will automatically be reciprocated in kind by our students?

If we provide feedback only at the end of learning, students don't have any meaningful opportunities to act on it. Unless we give them embedded and clearly directed time in class in which they are required to act on our feedback then all of that time we have spent marking may well be wasted and will have little visible impact. We must plan time within lessons or schemes of work where students act upon and consolidate the comments and feedback that we give them. As students easily forget or even ignore feedback, it also helps to actively get students to write their previous 'feedforward' targets on to any new work. Students therefore have the highlighted deficit from the last piece of work visible and in their mind when working on their new piece.

16. Deliberately set up productive failure

How do we keep raising the bar for our students?

Until we make the high level most challenging demands explicit we will never really know whether our students would have been capable of reaching the highest standards. In reality, we might all be guilty of the fact that some aspects of our teaching actually make it less likely that students are able to demonstrate what they are really able to do. By scaffolding their work too clearly (and for too long), we can undermine expectations and restrict the ranges of response that our students could potentially develop 'off the leash'. If we focus on continually making our deliberately signposted and increasingly challenging demands clear and are raising the bar through rigorous feedback to their extended and reasoned answers then we have an opportunity to see what they are really capable of achieving. At the same time, we need to teach them to expect and deal with failure. Only in this way can we begin to ensure that it is seen as productive failure by our students.

17. Explain the notion of desirable difficulties

How can we teach students to take personal responsibility and to persist in the face of obstacles?

Learning only really happens when we are subjected to cognitive strain, deliberately designed difficulty, as that is when we are required to fully concentrate. Introducing certain difficulties into the learning process can greatly improve long-term retention of the learned material. In psychology studies thus far, these difficulties have generally been modifications to commonly used methods that add an additional hurdle during the learning or studying process (Bjork, R.A., 1994). Strain is generally regarded as unpleasant and so we unconsciously try to avoid it. By routinely teaching around the obstacles we mislead our students into believing in an easy road to success. It becomes less bumpy when students accept that they are supposed to think hard, pay attention and struggle. Getting it wrong is not failure but progress and only when students are forced into failure do they fully understand this. Too many able students seem to think that effort is only for the inept, which can quickly lead to 'imposter syndrome', where a child never really believes that they are clever and thereby become way too reliant on externally given accreditation.

18. Plan in ambiguity, complexity and doubt

How do we encourage confusion endurance with the security that students sometimes need?

Puzzlement is a powerful way to enter into an enquiry. We need our students to actually engage with the stimulation of wrestling with unforeseen obstacles and problems, particularly if this involves anomalies that undermine comfortable assumptions. They need to know, and their teachers need to understand, that education is not only about finding the answers; just as exciting is finding the questions. We need to concentrate on what our subject still cannot answer and to understand why by examining why things are still uncertain. It helps to design deliberate disorientation into your lessons, to enable students to become defamiliarised and have to cope with (and make sense of) these experiences. Expose students to novel situations that might deliberately threaten their security and self-esteem, and offer them the opportunity to make disparate connections and to apply existing knowledge to new challenges. Only then will they feel a genuine enjoyment of ambiguity, complexity and uncertainty, speculating on what isn't there, what remains to be discovered.

19. Focus on threshold concepts

Where are the knotty bits in our subject and how can they best be presented to students?

It is a significant move to get students to think about what elements are critical and transformative to learn in a subject. But these tricky concepts that underpin our subject need to be offered to students in a form that doesn't short-circuit their own thinking (Land, Meyer, and Smith, 2008). Many of these concepts are complex and therefore progress will be messy rather than smooth and linear, and that gives us the greatest trouble in communicating them to classes without compromising their integrity and challenge. It has been argued that we learn most from the moments that jar, not from the moments that gel. In addition, the focus on the jarring moments will help us to strip back content and be less dependent on the constant changes to the curriculum. It is difficult for able students to genuinely appreciate what excellence and scholarship might look like if we insist on feeding them only the less complex elements. Instead we need to talk explicitly about subject mastery and not gloss over the big issues in our subject.

20. Share what makes you excited

What is emotionally engaging about your subject and why is it meaningful?

Students tend to apprentice themselves to us. It is sometimes easier to stretch and accelerate our more able students than it is to keep them on the journey with us. As teachers, we sometimes forget our love for our subject and that we have become experts. We get used to 'explaining' key concepts and the more difficult areas of our domains but we neglect to explain to our students what it is that we found emotionally engaging about our subject in the first place: Why we chose to study it and what we feel it is there to explain. So it is really helpful to use personal anecdotes, stories and epiphanies in our classroom to support our students to understand why it is meaningful. That includes making it clear that there are moments where we still get excited about our subject, and why that happens, by modelling genuine curiosity in our reactions to recent events or questions. It also means that we should explain to students what helped us to 'get' our subject, our own learning histories and where our sense of security and expertise comes from.

21. Establish a transformational culture

How do we encourage students on the road to expertise?

Critically, we can only do this by not being the only thinker and questioner in the classroom. We need to normalise and rigorously reinforce scholarship and try to make academic achievement and a love of learning more socially desirable. We need to celebrate expertise and mastery and normalise intellectual debate, specifically by talking about learning and studying as rewards in themselves. Even very simple ideas such as having students carrying reading books with them everywhere they go can boost their notions of personal possibility and scholarship. There are numerous aspects to any student's home life that can cause barriers to success but by immersing them in a world that celebrates academic learning, a school classroom culture can chip away at self-doubt. An effective school culture ensures that students are reminded of 'the best that they can be' in form rooms, corridors, lessons, assemblies and in every interaction with a teacher.

The well timed public support, the one to one conversations and positive parental feedbacks can also help to shift doubts by helping them to see themselves as high-achieving students, doing well and wanting to do even better. Once a student sees that they are capable of achieving excellence, it can be, and often is, transformational. They never see themselves in quite the same way again.

References

Bjork, R.A.: 'Memory and metamemory considerations in the training of human beings'; In J. Metcalfe & A. Shimamura (Eds.), *Metacognition: Knowing About Knowing*. Boston, MA: MIT Press 1994, pp. 185–205.

Land, R., Meyer, J.H.F. and Smith, J. (eds.): *Threshold Concepts Within the Disciplines*; Rotterdam, the Netherlands: Sense Publications 2008.

Rimm, S.: *Underachievement Syndrome: Causes and Cures*; Cupertino, CA: Apple Publishing, 1986.

Chapter 14

Glossary of ideas

Passport check?

Acceleration: This might mean 'fast-tracking' a student into an older age-group, or it might mean taking an examination earlier. It would be uncommon for a student to take *all* their lessons with an older group, or take more than a small number of their subject examinations early. Acceleration is most commonly used to describe different provision for particular aspects of a subject, rather than the whole course.

Character: Paul Tough dismisses the idea that character and traits are the same thing and as a result are unchanging. He defines character as: *a set of abilities or strengths that are very much changeable – entirely malleable, in fact. They are skills you can learn; they are skills you can practice; and they are skills you can teach* (2012). Angela Duckworth talks about character under two distinct headings: the ways it drives motivation and its importance as a generator of willpower and self-control: *no matter the domain, the highly successful had a kind of ferocious determination that played out in two ways. First, these exemplars were unusually resilient and hard-working. Second, they knew in a very, very deep way what it was they wanted. They not only had **determination**, they had **direction***. Tough says that character can act as a safety net for those students who have limited support from their families and surrounding culture, or who stand a greater chance of making wrong turnings and choices. Without the safety net of class, *you need more grit, more social intelligence, more self-control than wealthier kids* (2012). Tough, Dweck and Duckworth all see character as malleable rather than fixed, Dweck would go further and say that intelligence, like character, can 'grow' their intelligence, students can achieve more and do not have to settle for an immovable ceiling on their potential.

Co-construction: Students working confidently with their teachers to take increasing ownership of their own learning. They develop the independence to contribute to the content of their learning, its sequencing, how it is taught and assessed. In the business world, companies tend not to work when they operate in response to top-down answers; free markets work better because they are built on trial and error, they listen in order to add to their knowledge and they are able to grow because they are adaptable. In a classroom setting, Michael Barber called this adaptability **co-construction** – the idea that the learning process is about knowledge-building rather than knowledge transference: adults provide the scaffolding; learners are partners in what Syed calls an 'open loop' where feedback is used to transform failure into success. A 'closed loop' would be when failure is ignored or not acted upon.

Cognitive bandwidth: Knowing a little about a lot so that it is possible to use, adapt and compare a wide range of knowledge. This is Montaigne's idea that it is important to 'learn scatteringly'. Being able to call on a store of existing knowledge enables the learner to get more from new learning. The learner can compare new with existing knowledge and through that process, and open the universe, a little more.

Collaborative learning: Much of the recent research and commentary on effective learning, for example the Sutton Trust, John Hattie, or Carol Dweck, lays emphasis on three main factors:

1. Collaborative or reciprocal learning: in pairs or groups and involving peer tutoring and assessment.
2. Learning to learn – using the vocabulary of learning. In other words, learners having the words to describe the experiences they are going through and how they might fine-tune their responses to those experiences.
3. The ways in which adults (and peers) feedback/respond one to another and particularly to the work in hand.

Concerted cultivation: This idea comes from the American sociologist, Annette Lareau, writing in 2011. It's about nurturing and maximising a child's abilities through lots of activities and talk. A 1984 study by British researchers Tizard and Hughes found that the more questions a parent asked of their children, the more the children asked questions back. Question asking and question making not only generate talk and a rich relationship, they also activate learning.

Context principle: The way students behave – and learn and achieve – depends on personality *and* the situation. Students learn and react differently in different situations. There is no such thing, according to this view, as a person's 'essential nature'.

Cultural capital: The sociologist Pierre Bourdieu coined this phrase to describe the bedrock of knowledge that the powerful in any society share – which is why they send their children to exclusive schools where learning is traditional and teacher-led. The educational conservative E.D. Hirsch argues that a knowledge-rich curriculum is *the only means whereby children from disadvantaged homes can secure the knowledge and skills that will enable them to improve their condition* (2007). This interpretation of the phrase, cultural capital, implies a common core curriculum. On the other hand, the KIPP (Knowledge is Power Program) in the US found that although the teacher-led/core curriculum approach was successful in schools, the drop-out rate in university was unusually high – because those students didn't survive without close instruction and guidance, and being told what to think. This doesn't invalidate the importance of cultural capital in the way we think about individual school subjects. See the entry on 'threshold concepts'.

Déjà vu and **Vuja de**: *Déjà vu* is when we come across something new, but feel we have met it somewhere before. *Vuja de* is the opposite – we come across something familiar but we see it in a completely new way. This idea comes from Adam Grant, who describes *vuja de* as finding *a way to gain new insights into old problems* (2016).

Desirable difficulties: The phrase, 'desirable difficulties' comes from the American psychologist, Robert Bjork. His idea is that, *introducing certain difficulties into the learning process can greatly improve long-term retention* (2011). By introducing hurdles to surmount the learner is made to engage in *a deeper processing of material* with the result that long-term retention is improved. Bjork and others have identified some of the following ways of introducing 'desired difficulties':

- Spacing the learning sessions rather than grouping them together.
- Testing learners on materials rather than simply restudying it.
- Learners encouraged to generate their own target materials actively, rather than reading it passively.
- Varying the setting in which the learning takes place.
- Presenting learning materials in a less organised form.

Bjork talks about the difference between *retrieval strength*, which is when the learner acquires and learns some knowledge rapidly (for a test, say), and *storage strength*, which is the slow acquisition of knowledge. Making the learning easy and accessible can improve retrieval strength and enhance performance. His message, however, is that we should develop methods that enhance storage strength – or long-term retention – rather than emphasising short term performance.

Diversive curiosity: General inquisitiveness sometimes ignites learning, sometimes distracts from learning. The curious student can be wonderful to teach, the curious student whose interests are unchanneled can become a distraction.

Enrichment: This is about *breadth* and a broader, a wider (rather than necessarily deeper) understanding of a subject area; *additional* subject material, opportunities for comparisons, connections, wider contexts. For instance, making use of the concept of intertextuality in English or going on trips to museums for history or science. Learners might explore additional dimensions of the same topic, or an entirely new topic.

Epistemic (sometimes known as specific) curiosity: This is about a sustained exploration of a topic, of finding ways to get students to invest in an aspect of their learning over a period.

Equifinality: This idea comes from mathematics and maintains that there are many, equally valid, ways to reach the same outcome. Working from the belief that there are *always* multiple ways to get from one place to another, is sometimes called the *pathways principle*. The opposite of this is *normative thinking* – the belief that there is only one normal pathway from A to B.

Ergodic theory: This is about the relationship between groups and individuals. The average behaviour of a group predicts the behaviour of individuals – if every member of the group is identical and if every member of the group stays the same in the future. It's the mistaken assumption that you can understand individuals by ignoring their individuality. Some have used this as a way of explaining how schools have gone wrong.

Essentialist thinking: This is the belief that the identification of traits can uncover our essential wiring and get to the very heart of who we are. Once those traits are exposed we will be able to predict exactly how we will perform in any given situation. This is called *essentialist thinking* and it is both a *cause* and *a consequence of typing*. The context principle (above) challenges this view. Clearly, it's a nature versus nurture argument but then recent research (see *The Guardian* 23.5.17: 'Study Finds 40 new genes that affect intelligence') shows that 40 recently discovered genes could account for a 5% difference in IQ. Watch this space.

Experiential learning: Seeing the learning process as a cycle which looks something like this: 1. Concrete experience. 2. Observation and reflection. 3. The shaping of abstract ideas. 4. The testing of those ideas.

Extension: *Depth*, going deeper into an area of study; this idea invites *independent* learning and *collaboration*, and that means more than superficial co-operation (working nicely together), it means producing innovative ideas together. It also implies seeking to meet with out of school expertise, encounters and experiences. It might involve considering a topic from an unfamiliar perspective or it might foreground problem solving. Learners might need to acquire new knowledge and skills and may anticipate material that typically occurs later in the programme of study.

Failure: If I want to be a great musician, I must first play lots of bad music. If I want to become a great tennis player, I must first lose lots of tennis games. If I want to become a top commercial architect known for energy-efficient, minimalist designs, I must first design inefficient, clunky buildings (Babineaux and Krumboltz, 2014).

Successful people, in sport for instance, are not afraid of failure. They learn from failure, they adapt and grow. If our children live their lives entirely in a performance environment (of constant tests and assessments, for instance) where they believe they are not allowed to fail, they will become afraid of even trying. Thinking of the classroom as a practice rather than a performance environment helps, and using the idea of a pre-mortem – where students are asked to imagine the failure of a plan, a project, or a learning goal before it has even been put into action – is worth thinking about. The idea then is to articulate plausible reasons why the failure has happened. Sometimes called 'prospective hindsight' the intention is not to destroy learning intentions but rather to strengthen them.

Feedback: Students needs other voices and ideas if they are to continue to shape and develop their own perceptions and experiences. These other voices come in the form of feedback and the consensus is that those voices need to:

- Focus on the task, not the learner; to respond to the answer, the idea, the work, the activity – not the individual.
- Try to link the feedback to the goals of the session.
- Keep feedback specific, simple and focused; generate enough information to help the dialogue move on – and no more.

- Be aware that praise needs care: Dweck stresses how important it is to praise effort and use mistakes to build progress. It should be more about what is right than what is wrong, non-threatening and encouraging.
- Be careful not to suppress the wonder and the romance, the questions and the desire to know and get things right. Dumb questions and dumb answers can be starters to new perceptions and new answers.

Flow: This idea comes from psychologist Mihaly Csikszentmihayli and describes that state of complete and unreflective immersion is a topic or an activity that students experience when they are driven by interest rather than when they pursue goals and rewards (see Motivation). Some would argue that this is the source of true happiness.

The formation of attention: This is perhaps the neatest description of the teaching and learning process that we are likely to meet. It encapsulates that development from curiosity to discovery, discipline and independence that we hope all learners will experience. It is not about certainties but possibilities; neither is it about preconceptions but is rather about doubt. There is a related useful phrase: *the transformative power of attention* – from James Ward – which means making small things interesting by looking closely.

Grit: For Angela Duckworth (2016), developing character, or 'grit' comes down to the concept of *follow-through* – sticking with a goal over an extended period, showing continuous commitment. For her, a student's capacity to *practice grit* perhaps best finds expression in extracurricular activities. Duckworth reasons that children are often drawn to such activities out of interest, but that when the adult in charge gets it right, those activities provide an effective mix of support and challenge. As a result, the child experiences purpose, ambition, hope and the rewards of practice. It's a powerful combination of approaches: motivation and challenge. The outcome is the development of ability or character quality that enables a follow-through on a commitment. Providing or challenging young people with such activities not only invites the use of what Duckworth calls, 'grit' but also builds that quality.

Hard-thing rule: This is from Angela Duckworth again. Each student (and teacher/ teaching assistant) chooses a challenging (hard) thing that to achieve will require daily practice. The focus of their efforts is entirely self-chosen. Individuals can give up but only at a pre-agreed time – like the end of term. Duckworth says that this venture is *to encourage grit without obliterating the child's capacity to choose their own path* (2016).

Higher level thinking: in Bloom's taxonomy, this would be a level of thinking (or questioning) that goes beyond knowledge and recall, or comprehending and understanding, or analysing (breaking down into parts). When students use what they have learned to create something new (synthesise) or evaluate (judge according to a given set of criteria) then they are said to be moving towards higher level thinking. Similarly, Bloom and others would argue that this is a useful framework of questioning techniques, which for teachers might use to push individuals and groups to higher levels of thinking.

If-then signatures: This is about how the context influences the outcome. The question to ask isn't – why is this student not getting it, or why is this section of the course not working – but rather, why is this student not getting it *in this context* – or why is this part of the course failing to communicate itself *in this context?* In other words, the person and the situation are inextricably linked; things happen or do not happen out of the interaction between the two. Learning, and behaviour, in this reading of the process, are context specific.

The jaggedness principle: this is from Todd Rose and it is about individuality and how we cannot apply one-dimensional thinking to understand something that is complex – or 'jagged'. Jaggedness suggests multiple dimensions and at the same time, a degree, however slight, of some connection between those dimensions. Rose says that jaggedness *is about every human characteristic we care about- including talent, intelligence, character, creativity, and so on* (2017).

Mental contrasting: When it comes to thinking about **how** we can 'teach' a growth mindset – develop intelligence and character – Duckworth would say it's a matter of focusing on both motivation and volition at the same time. Wall-to-wall 'positive fantasising' as Duckworth calls it (about achieving your dreams of being rich and famous) are useless unless you can address the obstacles that make that ambition difficult. Duckworth and others have described a process which they call, *'mental contrasting'* which invites the student to think about the positive outcomes from their endeavours and contrast those thoughts against the obstacles that will make that achievement tricky (Duckworth, Kirby, Oettingen and Gollwitzer, 2009). Matthew Syed talks about the importance of 'redefining failure' if we are to achieve high performance. He quotes the Head of Wimbledon High School, London: *Our focus here is on failing well, on being good at failure. What I mean by this is taking the risk and then learning from it if it doesn't work* (2007).

Meta-cognitive strategies: learning about learning; thinking about thinking – like thinking out loud, pre-writing – planning work. It's about finding ways to 'drive the brain' towards independent learning.

Motivation: Two types: (1) *extrinsic motivation*: this is goal focused; work hard now in these ways and your reward will come in examination grades. This sort of motivation is usually generated by a third party, a parent or a teacher, but individuals can choose to set the goals for themselves. (2) *Intrinsic motivation* is about *interest*. It's an off-shoot of curiosity (see 'Flow').

Need for cognition (NFC): Scientists distinguish between individuals who want their inner life to be as simple as possible and those who derive pleasure and enjoyment from intellectual challenges. It's a measure of intellectual curiosity. Ian Leslie, in his book, *Curious: The Desire to Know and Why Your Life Depends on It* (2014) includes a questionnaire designed to assess individual NFC ratings.

Non-cognitive traits: character and personality are now taken seriously as key factors in educational achievement. *Attitudes* and *habits* are, if anything, seen as more important than intelligence when it comes to outcomes. Conscientiousness, persistence, self-discipline and Duckworth's 'grit' – and the way she highlights how important it is to be able to deal with failure – are all crucial. Sophie von Stumme would add that curiosity is a key characteristic because it more than any other quality, predicts of academic success. Curiosity combines intelligence with character – a hunger for novelty with persistence – and scientists would call this '*need for cognition*' (curiosity) a perfect match for conscientiousness. A hungry mind, she concludes, is the *third pillar of academic achievement* (von Stumme, Hell and Chamorro-Premuzic, 2011).

Normative thinking: there is only one normal route to achieving a goal. It's difficult to ignore the fact that this premise has done a good deal of damage – particularly in the field of health care and medicine. Yet quite a few teachers would base their approach to their work using the same benchmark. Called sometimes one-dimensional or essentialist thinking.

Pace: We should learn to question the pace of the learning that happens in our classrooms. To slow, and students lose interest; too fast and students lose track. We should question the assumption that faster suggests higher ability, and slower a lesser ability, and we have to ask if learning quickly means retaining is easier. It's that question, again, about whether you match the individual to the learning environment, or whether you allow the learning environment to embrace individuality.

'PISA shock': This is when a country's education system is plunged into crisis by the publication of that country's ranking by the Programme of International Student Assessment. The assessment measures mostly mathematics, reading and science, with a small amount of problem-solving and financial literacy. Many argue that since these assessments began, education systems across the world have dramatically increased their reliance on quantitative testing. Education has become about testing and finding ways to rise up the PISA rankings. We have become nations of league tables, some would argue, which are easy to sensationalise and which make unfair comparisons between very different societies. PISA assessments offer – *a single, narrow, biased yardstick* which runs the risk of harming the *great diversity of educational traditions and cultures*.

Priming the pump: According to George Lowenstein when we know something about a subject we want to know more; we are stimulated by a 'gap' in our knowledge. This is reminiscent of Michael Marland's observation that motivation is driven, most of all, by achievement. As Louise Pasteur said, *chance favours the prepared mind*. Teachers 'prime the pump' by stimulating and feeding curiosity.[1]

Productive frustration:

> Education . . . isn't only, or even primarily, about creating children who are proficient with information. It's about filling them with questions that ripen, via deferral, into genuine interests.
>
> (Greenman, 2010)

This is a warning to take care that when we close information gaps (via the internet, for instance) we must take care not to close down curiosity.

Puzzles and mysteries: Security expert Gregory Treverton (writing about the Enron disaster) said:

> If things go wrong with a puzzle, identifying the culprit is easy; it's the person who withheld information. Mysteries, though, are a lot murkier, sometimes the information we've been given is inadequate, and sometimes we aren't very smart about making sense of what we've been given, and sometimes the question itself cannot be answered. Puzzles come to satisfying conclusions. Mysteries often don't.
>
> (qtd. in Gladwell, 2010)

See the entry on 'desirable difficulties' – we learn better when we find the learning hard – or harder, at least.

Questions: Which approach? Asking questions that have a straightforward right or wrong answer? Asking questions that promote research? Asking questions where there isn't one answer but multiple, sometimes conflicting, answers? Asking questions that invite collaboration with others – including adults? Asking questions that lead to more questions? If the first type allows little room for discussion, the second type (where the learner is invited to go in search of the answer) has more possibilities. The fact that the answer is out there somewhere does not inhibit speculation and therefore imaginative engagement. The third type of question, where there is no fixed answer (yet), is about dialogue – stimulating what Piaget calls *cognitive conflict*.

Reciprocal learning: Group work – cited by several sources as one of the most effective approaches to learning. Using structured groupwork frequent assessment and teaching thinking and learning skills significantly raise outcomes (C4EO, 2011). Also named by Hattie and Claxton in their top three effective learning strategies.

Semantic contingency: This phrase comes from Catherine Snow. She writes about how children from poor families have difficulty learning to use language to describe things, construct arguments and solve abstract problems – in short, to use academic language. Some parents, not just the materially deprived, hear talk in their families that is almost entirely transactional: 'your dinner's ready'; 'put your clothes away'; 'time you went to bed' and so on. Business talk, which for the most part simply tells them what to do. In other, perhaps more middle-class families, the talk is what she calls, *semantically contingent* – parents respond to what the child says in ways which focus closely on the language the child has used, and in the process, draws attention to the variety of language and encourages higher levels of response. This sort of talk encourages reflection, conversation, extended responses, a greater variety of conversational formats and, in the end, more practice at finding the most effective ways to use communicate how we feel, what we need and what we believe.

Socratic questioning: In general, these are a progression of questions that invite enquiry – they 'progress' because they become increasingly challenging and abstract. The intention is to probe reasons and assumptions, to go into depth and to link *concepts* to observation and discussion. Robert Fisher (2009) illustrates the way Socratic questions might progress with, "What is a butterfly?" – to – "How does a butterfly differ from a bird?" – to – "So what defines an insect?".

Tension to learn: Not being satisfied is what makes finding out so satisfying. In the 1960s, H.I. Day devised what he called a, 'zone model of curiosity'. Psychologists use this model to illustrate the importance of a balance between an absence of curiosity and an excess of curiosity. If curiosity is missing, Day calls this a 'zone of relaxation' where motivation and the desire to explore are all but absent. If curiosity is too high, then a 'zone of anxiety' is the likely outcome – the person feels out of their depth, defensive and therefore avoids engagement. The perfect place to be, consequently, is what Day describes as the 'zone of curiosity'. George Lowenstein says, 'educators know more about educating motivated students than they do about motivating them in the first place'. At the heart of what he says is his contention that 'to stimulate curiosity, it is necessary to make students aware of the manageable gaps in their knowledge'. That word 'manageable' is crucial. If the gap between the knowledge they have and the knowledge we are offering appears to be too large, then the student will be overwhelmed and discouraged. If it is too small, then perhaps it's not worth the effort.

Burns and Gentry, in their 'Tension-to-Learn' Theory call this balance between what we know and what we'd like to know, a 'tension to learn'. It's about matching the 'manageable knowledge gaps' with the learner's natural curiosity. Susan Engel writes about how we do this.

Threshold concepts: Myer and Land define these as critical points when students make 'learning leaps', when they move their work beyond descriptive fact-finding to conceptual levels of understanding. These 'penny drop' moments represent leaps of faith beyond comfort zones when students acquire innovative ways of seeing, thinking and working. As a result, they experience conceptual paradigm shifts regarding their studies and themselves. How does a threshold concept work?

1. It is an idea, or a piece of information that is 'transformative'. It's a fresh perspective that involves a shift in understanding. It alters perception and leads the student into a different relationship with their subject and how they see themselves as a student. Once the new concepts are absorbed, that understanding is likely to be irreversable.
2. A second characteristic of a threshold concept is that it is 'integrative' – it exposes a previously hidden interrelatedness of one thing with another.
3. Threshold concepts may be 'bounded'. This means that they often lead to more questions than answers and therefore point towards new conceptual areas. They are not finite or fixed.
4. Perhaps a key idea in Meyer and Land's analysis is their contention that threshold concepts are often 'troublesome' – conceptually difficult, counter-intuitive or alien – and as a result require the student to jettison former ideas to absorb new ones – and this can be an emotional and challenging moment for them.
5. They are 'irreversible' – difficult to unlearn.
6. They invite a 'discursive' approach to learning – incorporating an enhanced and extended use of language.

7. Threshold concepts occupy a 'liminal' space in the learning process. They represent crossing points or a rite of passage. The writer, Frank O'Connor would call these 'frontier moments' where the student is part way towards mastery, oscillating between old and new understanding and not yet there. It is worth mentioning here that Myer and Land make some useful points about a default position which they call 'mimicry', where real understanding is substituted with ritualised performance: learning by rote, copying, taking 'refuge' in reciting knowledge rather than using it.

Traits: Essentialist thinkers believe that success in education is about our DNA, who we are deep down, our personality. A glance back through the twentieth century will show just how enthusiastically this idea has been taken up. There are scores of personality and trait based assessments being used by employers – notably the Myers–Briggs Type Indicator (MBTI), which categorises personality into sixteen types, and the Enneagram test, which identifies nine. It's a huge industry. Traits theory believes that we are all born with an inbuilt ladder that dictates how we are going to develop: our DNA predestines our development.

Webs of development: This is an alternative to those ladders of development and its proponent Kurt Fischer proposes that as we progress we are faced with alternatives – webs of development from which we choose the way forward. We are not hardwired for success or failure.

Note

1 Pasteur is quoted by Ian Leslie in *Curious*; Quercus 2014. The phrase 'priming the pump' has been around since the nineteenth century and was in common usage at the time of the Great Depression (by Hoover and Roosevelt). In more recent times, Donald Trump claims to have invented the phrase.

References

Bjork, R.A.: 'Desirable Difficulties in the Classroom'; *Psychology in Action* 2011.

Duckworth, Angela: *Grit: The Power of Passion and Perseverance*; London: Vermilion 2016.

Duckworth, Kirby, Oettingen and Gollwitzer: 'Mental Contrasting' *Journal of Applied Developmental Psychology* 2009.

Gladwell, M.: *What the Dog Saw*; London: Penguin 2010.

Greenman, B.: 'The Internet as Curiosity Machine'; *The Atlantic* 2010.

Hirsch, E.D.: *The Knowledge Deficit*; Boston, MA: Houghton Mifflin Harcourt 2007.

Leslie, I.: *Curious*; London: Quercus 2014.

Rose, T.: *The End of Average*; London: Penguin 2017.

Syed, M.: *Bounce: The Myth of Talent and the Power of Practice*; London: Fourth Estate 2011.

Tough, P.: *How Children Succeed; Grit, Curiosity and the Hidden Power of Character*; London: Random House 2012.

von Stumme, S., Hell, B. and Chamorro-Premuzic, T.: 'The Hungry Mind: Intellectual Curiosity is the Third Pillar of Academic Performance'; *Perspectives on Psychological Science* 2011.

Index

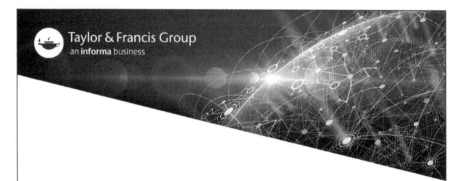

Printed in Great Britain
by Amazon